COUNTRY ROADS
Rockbridge County, Virginia

Katherine Tennery
Shirley Scott

Rockbridge Publishing Company
Berryville, Virginia

Published by

Rockbridge Publishing Company
Post Office Box 351
Berryville, VA 22611
Telephone; 703-955-3980
Facsimile: 703-291-4126

Library of Congress Cataloging-in-Publication Data

Tennery, Katherine, 1941-
    Country roads.

    Includes bibliographical references.
    1. Automobile travel—Virginia—Rockbridge
County—Guide-books. 2. Rockbridge County (Va.)—Description
and travel—Guide-books. 3. Rockbridge County (Va.)—History.
I. Scott, Shirley, 1922-   . II. Title.
    GV1024.T38   1989
    917.55'852
ISBN 0-9623572-0-0 (first edition)
ISBN 1-883522-05-6 (second edition)   89-10867
                                                          CIP

10 9 8 7 6 5 4 3 2 1
Second Edition (revised 1995)

Acknowledgments

A bevy of wonderful folks gave generously of their time and energy to help make these tours accurate and easy to follow. Others shared their local knowledge to help up bring historic Rockbridge to life. We appreciate their enthusiastic support!

Special thanks to Phyllis Bennington, Willetta Bennington, Hazel Bernard, D.E. Brady, Myra Brush, Johnny Buck, Liz Butler, Colonel and Mrs. William F. Byers, Phyllis Cartwright, Marion Chappell, Catherine Clayton, Brenna and Rachel Cothran, Janet Cummings, Mary Frances Cummings, Michael, Sara, Lee and Ryan Cunningham, K.H. Dunlap, Joseph Dunn, Helene Edwards, Loraine Ennis, Nancy and Stewart Epley, Alta Fowler, John Harb, Susan Harb, Carol Harlow, Ann Harris, Danta Harris, Jen Heffelfinger, Hester Holland, Lita D. and Bion Howard, Marilyn Hyatt, Sara M. Lewane, Sally Lewis, Colonel and Mrs. Arthur Lipscomb, Icer and Stuart Litvin, Grace McCrowell, Mary McFadden, Mary Miller, Josephine Morrison, Gertrude Neff, Nelson and Linda Norford, Edna Pickral, Karen Powell, Joan Robins, Mort M. Robins, Emily L. Sisler, Eric Sisler, Alex Skidmore, Nancy Parsons Skidmore, Anne Sauder, Donna M. Spears, Virginia and Phil Toale, Anne Tucker, Charles W. Turner, Margaret and Emery Wallin, Sue Watson, Adrian Whiteside, Gary Wilsher, Pat and Herb Winans, and Eleanor Wurzburger.

We are indebted to the Rockbridge Historical Society and the Ruth Anderson McCulloch Branch of the Association for the Preservation of Virginia Antiquities. Their publications were invaluable.

And **very special thanks** to Beth and Joe Thompson of the Best Seller and Vicki and Tom Perry of Mountain Copy-Graphics for extraordinary support and encouragement.

More Acknowledgments

When this book was first published in 1989, numbers identified the county roads, with an occasional traditional but unofficial road name. In the early 1990s the county board of supervisors elected to establish county-wide emergency 911 service, which required every road to have a name. The text of this edition has been revised to include those names, thanks in great part to the diligence of Winifred Hadsel, who painstakingly traced the history of the 369 new road names and presented them in *Roads of Rockbridge County,* published by the Rockbridge Historical Society in 1993. Her diligent efforts made possible the revision of this guidebook from afar.

In the course of the five years since the first edition, changes besides road names have occurred in the county—old bridges were replaced with new, country stores closed, old buildings disappeared, new enterprises sprang up. To document these changes, a new bevy of test drivers hit the road, and to them is due very special thanks indeed.

The second wave of test drivers included Janet Coleman, Alta Fowler, James and Toni Manuel, Josephine Morrison, Ned and Barbara Reister, Susan and Anita Risener, Mark Robinson, Bea Tharp, Jean Wolfe and Dorsey and Jean Woodson.

Special thanks to all of you!

Contents

Introducing Rockbridge County

Situated in the Great Valley of Virginia, bounded by the Blue Ridge on the east and the Allegheny Mountains on the west, Rockbridge County, Virginia, is one of the most beautiful places in the United States. Its elevation tempers its climate; its geography encompasses imposing hills and gentle valleys, deep forests, windswept meadows, and clear streams that tumble down rocky slopes to unite in broad, rolling rivers. Peaceful farms, churches, and villages contribute a feeling of friendliness and serenity in harmony with the beauty of the land.

Long before the Europeans arrived, roaming Indians had worn paths, often wide enough to accommodate a wagon, through the valley. Their main route, known early on as the Pennsylvania Road, developed into the Valley Turnpike, a part of the Great Wilderness Road that opened present-day West Virginia, Kentucky, and Tennessee to settlement. Today we follow that same general route on US 11 and I-81. The Midland Trail (now US 60) brought settlers from Virginia's Tidewater region.

A Little History

There were settlers in this part of the Great Valley (near Staunton, in Augusta County) as early as 1732. In 1737 Benjamin Borden arrived in what is now Rockbridge County bearing a grant from Virginia's Governor Gooch for 92,100 acres of the Crown's land. (Borden, like so many of the county's present newcomers, came from New Jersey.) Since the Governor's purpose was to develop this rugged wilderness, the grant required that Borden settle a hundred families on the the land within a year. He advertised, and the settlers came, most of them stern, hardy, God-fearing Scotch-Irish families who, finding Pennsylvania already crowded, moved on to this new frontier.

Rockbridge County was created from parts of sprawling Augusta and Botetourt counties by an act passed by the Virginia Assembly in 1777. The act decreed that a court be established and located as close to the center of the county "as the situation and convenience shall admit. And ... that at the place which shall be appointed for holding court ... there shall be laid off a town ... 1300 feet in length and 900 in width." Lexington's name honors Lexington, Massachusetts, where the first battle of the Revolution had taken place two years before. The Natural Bridge, one of the Seven Natural Wonders of the Modern World, gave the county its name.

Like other pioneer regions, Rockbridge County was largely self-sustaining in its early decades. Farmers supplied food for themselves and the townsfolk. Mills were built to grind wheat and corn, and settlements grew around the mills, with blacksmith shops and general stores. Sturdy log buildings were erected to serve as churches and/or schools—and as refuges from occasional Indian attacks.

The Civil War wreaked havoc here as elsewhere. The post-war years brought a short-lived economic boom as developers tried to take advantage of the valley's iron and tin ore and abundant limestone. The arrival of railroads and the growth of Lexington's two great colleges—Washington & Lee University and the Virginia Military Institute—and Southern Virginia College for Women in Buena Vista spurred the county's growth. So also did the development of spas, attracting people from far-distant cities to enjoy the clear mountain air and mineral springs.

Rockbridge Today

About 18,000 people now live in Rockbridge County's 601.6 square miles, with an additional 13,000 almost equally divided beween the two cities of Lexington and Buena Vista. The county's rugged, rock-strewn landscape and limestone soil have dictated its best use: 17 square miles belong to the Jefferson and Washington national forests; more acres are set aside as part of the Blue Ridge Parkway and for the State Game Commission's Lake Robertson and two wildlife management areas. Much of the remainder serves as range for cattle, horses, and sheep. An early visitor, the Reverend Robert Rose, wrote in 1751 that "Providence designed this County for pasturage." Many of the villages that once dotted the county have all but disappeared.

Roaming Rockbridge

Natural Bridge, the caverns, the colleges, and Lexington's well-maintained historic district attract many visitors. And many of them arrive via the interstate and depart the same way, unaware that they have missed the essence of Rockbridge County—the enticing variety of its natural beauty and the many fascinating remnants of its history.

Come out into the county and explore! This guide describes 18 excursions, each with its own detailed map; all are shown on the master map inside the front cover. Most of the routes begin in or near Lexington. Some form a loop, bringing you back to where you began; others seem to end in the middle of nowhere, but actually connect with another route.

All you need for a pleasant afternoon of exploration is this guide and a sense of adventure. We suggest that you read through the tour description before setting out; you may find you will want to take along binoculars, a picnic, swimming togs, or hiking boots.

Since most Rockbridge roads radiate from Lexington or its vicinity, you needn't worry about getting lost. If you get confused, you can always go back the way you came. In fact, you may want to drive a route in both directions; you'll find the return journey a different drive altogether.

Routes designated US (US 60, US 11) are federal highways. Those with a VA prefix (VA 39, VA 56) are Virginia primary highways. Those with an SR designation are state secondary roads. Unless otherwise noted in the text, all are paved.

> A NOTE ABOUT MILEAGE: The mileage figure provided at the head of each tour is the length of that excursion, in one direction. It does not include the miles from your starting point to the beginning of the trip, nor the return from the end of the trip. Be sure to include those miles in your planning.

As you drive, stay alert for deer and other wildlife, stray livestock, or farmers moving machinery to another field. Control your interstate urges and heed the speed limits. The highway engineers did not allow any slack when they posted the curves—if the sign says 20 mph, believe it. If traffic builds behind you, pull over and let them pass.

Be particularly alert during and after a rain; the county's myriad springs, runs, creeks, and rivers can quickly flood a road. Some low-water bridges (noted in the text) are designed to go under regularly.

> When you stop to enjoy a view, study a structure, or read this guide, please remember that if you leave the road, you are probably on private property. The land and buildings are not open to the public.

Before you leave town, a quick check of the local papers *(The News-Gazette, The Weekender,* and *The Advocate)* will alert you to carnivals, sheepdog trials, cakewalks, auctions, horse shows, oyster dinners, and other events out in the county. Plan to join in the fun!

There are, of course, many more roads in the county than we cover here. We hope you will go beyond the scope of this book in your own exploration and that you will share your adventures with us.

And finally, as you drive, wave to the folks in oncoming vehicles; it's an old Rockbridge custom.

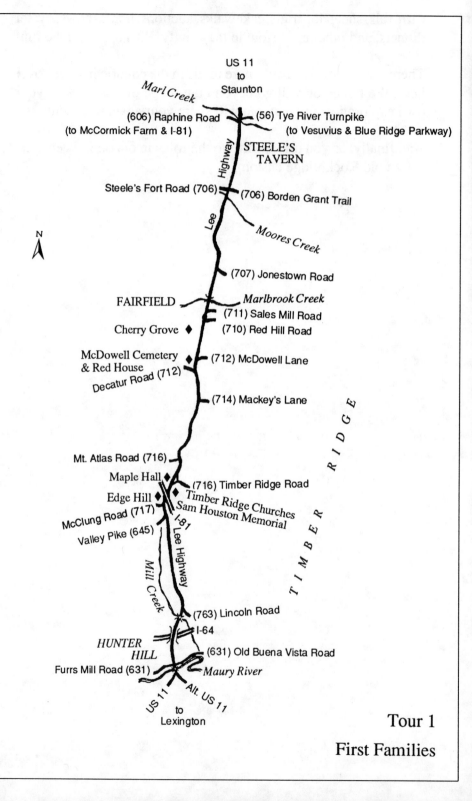

US 11
to
Staunton

Marl Creek

(606) Raphine Road
(to McCormick Farm & I-81)

(56) Tye River Turnpike
(to Vesuvius & Blue Ridge Parkway)

STEELE'S
TAVERN

Lee Highway

Steele's Fort Road (706)

(706) Borden Grant Trail

Moores Creek

(707) Jonestown Road

FAIRFIELD

Marlbrook Creek

(711) Sales Mill Road

Cherry Grove ◆

(710) Red Hill Road

McDowell Cemetery
& Red House

(712) McDowell Lane

Decatur Road (712)

(714) Mackey's Lane

Mt. Atlas Road (716)

Maple Hall ◆

(716) Timber Ridge Road

Edge Hill ◆

Timber Ridge Churches
Sam Houston Memorial

McClung Road (717)

Valley Pike (645)

I-81

Lee Highway

Mill Creek

T I M B E R   R I D G E

(763) Lincoln Road

I-64

*HUNTER
HILL*

(631) Old Buena Vista Road

Furrs Mill Road (631)

Maury River

US 11

Alt. US 11

to
Lexington

Tour 1

First Families

Lexington to Steele's Tavern
via Lee Highway: 16 Miles

This drive takes you further into local history than any other route in Rockbridge County. Evidence of the importance of religion, education, and family to the pioneers who settled the area abounds in old churches, schools, and homes. Memorials honor Rockbridge sons who gained fame on other frontiers.

The Robert E. Lee Highway (US 11), heads northward on a broad, often divided, modern road through Fairfield to the Rockbridge/Augusta county line in Steele's Tavern.

FROM LEXINGTON, go north on Main Street (one-way north in the historic downtown area), and across the bridge over the Maury River. You are now on Lee Highway. Ahead of you is **Hunter Hill**.

In June 1864, Union forces commanded by Major General David Hunter came over this hill as they attacked Lexington. During a three-day occupation of the city the Union army burned private homes and the Virginia Military Institute and destroyed the mills and iron furnaces that were supplying the Confederacy.

Although Hunter was driven back to the Ohio River by General Jubal Early soon after this siege, his deep penetration into Confederate territory foreshadowed the eventual outcome of the war.

At the top of Hunter Hill, near the College Square shopping center, the road becomes a four-lane divided highway, then descends to cross I-64 and wend its way north along **Timber Ridge**.

The series of low ridges that parallel Lee Highway north of Lexington are known collectively as Timber Ridge. In the 1730s, dense forests covered these ridges. The pioneers cleared the land to plant crops, and today much of Timber Ridge lies in cultivated fields or pastures.

The earliest landowners in what is now Rockbridge County—the Borden, McDowell, and Greenlee families—settled in this area. Ephraim McDowell and John Mackey vie for the honor of being the first settler on Timber Ridge; Mackey arrived in 1727, ten years before McDowell, but being a hunter who moved about, did not file a homestead claim until after McDowell.

Six miles north of Lexington is a small cluster of motels and restaurants near the I-81 overpass. On the left, just beyond the Days Inn, stands **Edge Hill**. Turn left onto McClung Road (717) for a look.

A private home tucked away in a little hollow, Edge Hill was built in the early 1800s, with substantial additions made in 1866. It perches halfway up the hill, overlooking tiny Mill Creek and scattered outbuildings. Except for one brief period, Edge Hill has housed successive generations of the Campbell-Alexander-Lyle family since 1825.

McClung Road (a one-lane gravel road that follows the creek) is named in honor of the five generations of an old Rockbridge family who once lived along here.

Back on Lee Highway, just beyond the I-81 overpass, stately **Maple Hall** commands your attention.

With its imposing, large-scale portico and double stairway, this Greek Revival Style house (1850) was specifically designed, tradition claims, to outshine its neighbors. Built by John Gibson, a local merchant, it now serves as a bed-and-breakfast inn with a public dining room.

Within sight of Maple Hall, on the right, a large sign identifies the **Sam Houston Memorial Wayside**. Pull into the small parking area in the welcoming, shady dell (with picnic tables) to visit the memorial.

A bronze plaque here reads:

Birthplace of Sam Houston

On March 2, 1793, the noted soldier and statesman Sam Houston was born in a log cabin on a nearby knoll. Houston served with distinction in the U.S. Army and later as a congressman and governor of Tennessee before moving to Texas in the 1830s. In Texas, he soon became a leader in the revolution against the Mexican government under General Antonio Lopez de Santa Anna. A signer of the Texas declaration of independence on March 2, 1836, Houston was chosen commander-in-chief of the Texian army. On April 21, 1836, he led his forces to victory in the battle of San Jacinto, which resulted in the independence of Texas.

Sam Houston twice served as president of the Republic of Texas. Later, after Texas became part of the United States of America, he served as US Senator and as governor. He died at his home in Huntsville, Texas, on July 26, 1863, during the Civil War, a struggle he bitterly opposed.

An able general, a strong political leader, and a friend to the Cherokee Indians who knew him as "The Raven", Sam Houston represented the true spirit of his native Virginia and his adopted states of Tennessee and Texas.

At the north end of the wayside is an historical marker for **Liberty Hall Academy**.

This school, from which Washington & Lee University evolved, occupied a log building near here in the late 18th century. The academy moved to Lexington, but the original building, which no longer exists, still served as a school; Sam Houston attended intermittently between 1801 and 1807.

From the wayside you can walk or drive up the hill to the two churches, an 1866 home, and a cemetery.

The **Timber Ridge Presbyterian Church** was organized in 1746. The original part of this native limestone building was erected in 1756, making it the only colonial-era Presbyterian church still in use in the country. The structure has undergone many changes.

The cemetery on the far side of the church includes the grave of John Mackey, one of the first settlers.

Mackey (also written McKy) died in 1773; his remains lie beneath three stones—head stone, foot stone, and coffin-shaped slabstone—which give the impression of a bed in shape. Many early graves had slabstones, probably to protect them from animals.

Mackey's epitaph reads:

Remamber• Man•as•you•pass•by•
As•you•Are•Now•so•once•was •i•
As•i•Am•Now•you•soon•will•be•
Therefore•Think•on•Eternity

The stone is signed: NETHANIAL-EVINS, BULDER. Evins was a local farmer who carved gravestones as a sideline. It was not unusual for gravestones to be signed, and the stonecutter often gave his address as well.

The imposing mansion behind the cemetery is **Church Hill**.

Although the house is near the stone church, it was built by The Reverend Horatio Thompson, pastor of the brick church across the road. Constructed in 1866 in the Greek Revival Style popular at the time, the house is a Registered Virginia Landmark.

The **Associate Reformed Presbyterian (ARP) Church**, a sturdy, red brick structure, is just below the stone church.

> This congregation was established in 1778 and met in various places until 1814, when the two congregations began to share the stone building, using it on alternate Sundays. A dispute in 1855 prompted the ARP congregation to build their own church in a style quite different from that of the stone building.

You can get back on Lee Highway from the wayside, or drive a quarter mile past the brick church on Timber Ridge Road (716) to return to the highway.

About two miles north of the wayside, on the opposite side of the highway, are three points of interest: the 200-year-old **Red House**, the **McDowell Family Cemetery**, and the **Ephraim McDowell memorial**. Cross the median strip and double back if you want a closer look.

> John McDowell surveyed Benjamin Borden's grant in exchange for a thousand acres of it. In 1737 McDowell built the first Red House on this site, using peeled logs which were then stained with red ochre. A captain in the local militia, McDowell was killed in an Indian battle in 1742. In 1783 Joseph Treavy bought the house and tore it down to build an inn, the Federal Style Red House you see today (the portico is a 20th-century addition). This inn was a popular stage stop for many years.

> McDowell's younger son, Samuel, a colonel in the Army of the Revolution and a member of the Virginia legislature, lived in the original Red House with his family; Samuel's

son Ephraim, born there in 1771, became a surgeon and performed the world's first ovariotomy (page 107). A memorial to Dr. Ephraim McDowell, the Father of Abdominal Surgery, stands beside the road.

In the field north of the house is the brick-walled McDowell Cemetery. It is not open to the public. The obelisk that rises above the other monuments is dedicated to Captain McDowell and his grandson, James McDowell, Jr., who was the governor of Virginia from 1843 to 1846. The seven settlers killed in the Indian battle with McDowell are also buried here (page 59).

Return to the northbound lanes and drive a mile to **Cherry Grove**. The house is on the opposite side of the road; again, cross the median strip and double back for a good view.

Cherry Grove, home of James McDowell (Captain John McDowell's elder son), was built about 1790. The large frame house sits back from the road amid spacious lawns. James McDowell, Jr., was born here. His sister Elizabeth was married in this house to Thomas Hart Benton, who later represented Missouri in the US senate; their daughter married General John C. Frémont, who was instrumental in adding much of the west, especially California, to the growing nation.

About a half mile farther north the road narrows as it enters **Fairfield**. Lee Highway through town is fairly busy by local standards, and there are often vehicles parked on both sides of the street.

Fairfield is a quiet little town with several antique shops, a couple of churches, and an old cemetery, all strung along Main Street (Lee Highway). Some of the most interesting buildings are noted here.

Fairfield Presbyterian Church, just beyond the cemetery, was established in 1840 and moved into this Greek Revival style building in 1852. The cemetery belongs to the church.

Across the road and a little to the north stand two houses side by side, one brick and one stone. The brick house was built in 1827; it has an interesting moulded-brick cornice. The stone house is older, having been built about 1795 by Charles McAlister, the town's founder. The undressed pine trunks used to support the porch roof are 20th century additions.

Anchoring the north end of town, on the right side of the road, is the **Fairfield United Methodist Church**, an imposing white structure built in 1916-1917. Fairfield was a Methodist preaching point in the early 1800s.

Continue on Lee Highway for about four and a half miles, past the Blue Ridge Recreation Park, to the junction with Raphine Road (606), which marks the outskirts of **Steele's Tavern**.

An historical marker here is dedicated to local inventors: Cyrus McCormick (reaper) and J.A.E. Gibbs (chain-stitch sewing machine). The McCormick Farm (page 34) is about half mile west on Raphine Road and open to the public free of charge.

Steele's Tavern straddles Marl Creek and the Rockbridge/Augusta county line. It takes its name from David Steele, a colorful innkeeper here in the late 1700s. Wounded in the Revolutionary War, Steele bore a long scar on his face and a silver plate in his skull. The tavern, which no longer exists, was as much a source of information as refreshment; long benches stood outside, inviting travelers to sit a spell and share their news. Located about halfway between Lexington and Staunton, the village was for a while called Midway.

An historical marker near the creek notes the first pioneer encampment in 1737. It was here that Benjamin Borden met John McDowell and arranged with him to survey Borden's land grant.

This tour ends at Steele's Tavern; Tour 3 begins here. Raphine Road will take you to an I-81 interchange about a mile and a half to the west if you want a quick return to Lexington. There is a coffee shop near the interchange, and a service station.

Staunton is about 18 miles farther north on Lee Highway.

Lexington to Steele's Tavern
via South River Road: 20 miles

South River Road (608) crosses the northeastern quadrant of the county, closely following South River at the base of the Blue Ridge. From the earliest years of European settlement this valley attracted pioneers because of its rich farmland and forest, abundant water, and the iron and tin ore found in its slopes. A century ago the coming of the railroad and ambitious schemes for industrial development fostered hopeful little communities along the road. The economic boom failed, but the communities endure.

FROM LEXINGTON, head north on Main Street to the traffic light just across the Maury River bridge. Turn right onto Old Buena Vista Road (631), following the river.

> The handsome brick mansion on your left is **Clifton**. Built in the early 19th century, this manor house was named for its view of the river cliffs.

The Maury from here loops southward toward Buena Vista, and Old Buena Vista Road continues into open, rolling farmland, after passing under I-81. A VMI facility, **McKeathan Park,** is on the right, at the top of the hill beyond the overpass.

> The park contains the school's observatory, which is sometime open to the public by invitation, and a skeet range

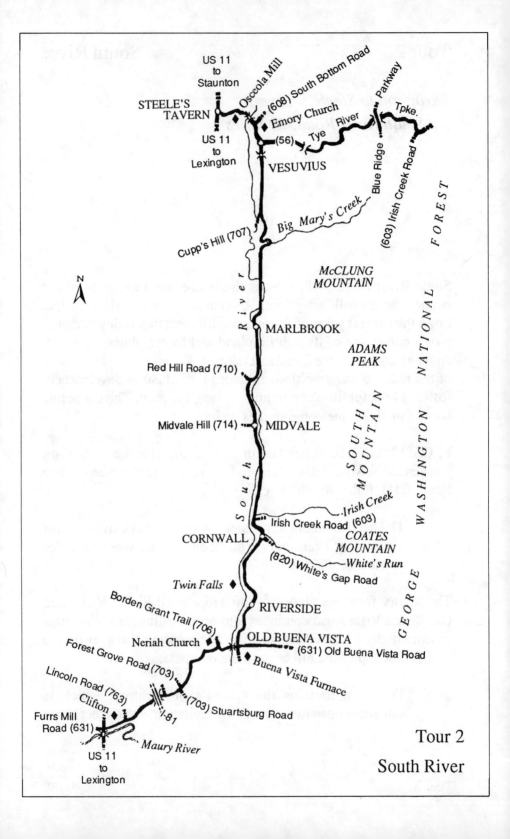

US 11
to
Staunton

STEELE'S
TAVERN

Osceola Mill

(608) South Bottom Road

Emory Church

Tye

River

Parkway

Tpke.

US 11
to
Lexington

(56)

VESUVIUS

Blue Ridge

(603) Irish Creek Road

WASHINGTON

NATIONAL

FOREST

Big Mary's Creek

Cupp's Hill (707)

McCLUNG
MOUNTAIN

River

MARLBROOK

ADAMS
PEAK

Red Hill Road (710)

South

SOUTH
MOUNTAIN

Midvale Hill (714)

MIDVALE

N

Irish Creek

Irish Creek Road (603)

CORNWALL

COATES
MOUNTAIN

White's Run

(820) White's Gap Road

GEORGE

Twin Falls

RIVERSIDE

Borden Grant Trail (706)

OLD BUENA VISTA

(631) Old Buena Vista Road

Neriah Church

Forest Grove Road (703)

Buena Vista Furnace

Lincoln Road (763)

Clifton

(703) Stuartsburg Road

I-81

Furrs Mill
Road (631)

Maury River

US 11
to
Lexington

Tour 2

South River

and picnic areas for use by VMI alumni, faculty and staff.

About a mile beyond the overpass, pull over and look back to enjoy a sweeping view of the valley.

Brushy Hill (1,955 feet), the twin peaks of House Mountain (3,645 and 3,386 feet), Hogback (2,542 feet), and the distant Alleghenies that form the western wall of the Valley of Virginia (the "Allegheny Front").

The name *Allegheny* is thought to be derived from an Indian word meaning endless. Its spelling is even less certain: Maryland and New York each have an *Allegany* County; the Virginia county is *Alleghany*; and the mountain range is *Allegeny*.

In another mile, on the left, stands **Neriah Baptist Church**.

Built in 1816 by John Jordan, Neriah has been in continuous use longer than any other Baptist church in the county. Most of this region's early settlers were Presbyterians. The handful of Baptists who formed the Neriah congregation decided that their building ought to be as imposing and impressive as any Presbyterian church—and so it is.

The Old Buena Vista Road turns sharply to the right at the church. In less than half a mile you will make the first of several crossings of South River. Just beyond the bridge is the intersection with South River Road (608).

The community here, Mountain View, also known as Old Buena Vista, includes a grocery store and an elementary school. Pull into the store's parking lot to get oriented.

South River seldom floods, but in August 1969 raging torrents swept away homes, bridges, and people. Floodwaters reached to the school, a quarter mile away.

That flood badly damaged the hitherto well-preserved remnants of the Buena Vista Furnace, which you can see across the road. Built in 1847-48, this once-thriving iron furnace is thought to have been named in honor of the American victory in the Mexican War's battle of Buena Vista. In 1864, General Hunter and his Union soldiers burned the furnace, and it was never restored.

As you leave the store, turn right onto South River Road. You are now heading north, following South River and the Norfolk Southern railroad tracks. For most of this trip the river marks the western boundary of the **George Washington National Forest**, which extends to the Blue Ridge (on your right).

Two treats enliven this stretch of flat bottomland. About a mile and a half along, at the dumpster site on the left, a pedestrian bridge crosses the river to homes on the other side. A sign sternly warns you not to make this narrow suspension bridge sway, but sway it does—with every step. A little farther along, just past the community of **Riverside**, on the left, **Twin Falls** plunges dramatically into the river. The property is privately owned; enjoy the view from your car.

In another half mile you will arrive at **Cornwall**.

This 1880s boomtown was named for Cornwall, England, which was then famous for its tin mines. Ownership disputes and the 1890s depression ended tin-mining operations here. (The mines in England are likewise largely defunct.) Sawmills also thrived here, until the accessible ridges were shorn bare. The trees you see are mostly second growth.

As you leave Cornwall, the road goes under a railway bridge, and the tracks and the river are both on your left. In another six tenths of a mile, note the junction with Irish Creek Road (603) (the end of

Tour 3) and the bridge over Irish Creek, which, after its long journey down the Blue Ridge slopes, here adds its substantial flow to South River.

> The next four to five miles take you through **Midvale** and **Marlbrook** and several crossings of the river. Then suddenly the road makes a hairpin turn and you have left the bottomlands to ascend a cool, wooded mountain ridge.

About a mile and a half after beginning the ascent is the road to a camp operated by the Virginia Federation of Garden Clubs.

> Campers study nature in a hands-on program of lessons learned for life. Several alumni, in fact, have subsequently distinguished themselves in the field of ecology.

Another mile and a half brings you to the outskirts of **Vesuvius**, once famous for its ironworks of the same name. When you reach the Tye River Turnpike (56), consider turning right to visit the Blue Ridge Parkway and Irish Creek (Tours 3 and 18), but heed the warnings on the large sign just across the tracks against the nature of this sometimes steep road.

Bear left on the Tye River Turnpike. In half a mile, on the right, is **Emory United Methodist Church**.

> Formed in 1808, the congregation first built a log church and then, in 1872, this simple but appealing frame building.

Beyond the church, you will cross the South River for the last time on this tour. The sizable gray building on the other side of the bridge was built in 1878 as **Osceola Mill**, which continued grinding corn and flour into the 1960s. The mill, along with the miller's house (1873) across the road, now serves as an elegant country inn.

Just past the mill, on the left, are the double cascades of Marl Creek's **Glenn Falls** (privately owned). The road winds sharply upward for a mile, to Lee Highway (US 11), the end of this journey, at the Rockbridge/Augusta county line in Steele's Tavern. Turn left on Lee Highway to return to Lexington (Tour 1, backwards, about 16 miles). Or consult the master map for other options.

Irish Creek Road from Tye River Turnpike
to South River Road: 20 miles

Here are mountains indeed! A bold sign warns that Tye River Turnpike (VA 56) is NOT RECOMMENDED FOR THRU TRUCKS. We would add that it is also not recommended for passenger cars without good brakes, plenty of power, and a stout-hearted driver. Beyond Vesuvius the road is wide, well-surfaced, and well-engineered, but it climbs and falls and twists mercilessly as it struggles to cross the Tye River Gap through the Blue Ridge. If you can cope, the scenery is well worth it, and you will be rewarded with a leisurely and undemanding journey down Irish Creek Road (603) as it meanders along beside Irish Creek.

This tour begins at Steele's Tavern (about 18 miles north of Lexington), goes east on Tye River Turnpike, then heads south on Irish Creek Road to end at the junction with South River Road (608) about 7 miles north of Lexington.

FROM LEXINGTON, go north on Lee Highway (US 11) to Steele's Tavern (Tour 1, about 18 miles) and turn right onto Tye River Turnpike. The last few paragraphs of Tour 2 describe this road through Vesuvius. Outside Vesuvius, note the sign marking the boundary of the **George Washington National Forest**.

You will be within the national forest for the remainder of this excursion, although the boundary does encompass

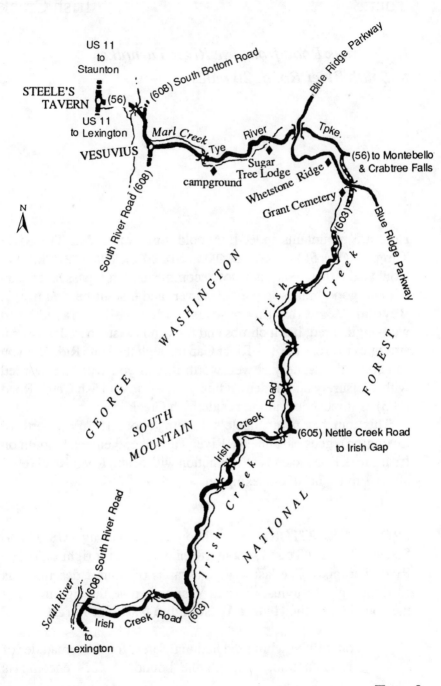

US 11
to
Staunton

STEELE'S
TAVERN (56)

US 11
to Lexington

VESUVIUS

(608) South Bottom Road

Marl Creek

Tye River

Tpke.

Blue Ridge Parkway

(56) to Montebello
& Crabtree Falls

Sugar
Tree Lodge

campground

Whetstone Ridge

Grant Cemetery

South River Road (608)

(603)

Blue Ridge Parkway

N

GEORGE WASHINGTON

Irish Creek

FOREST

SOUTH MOUNTAIN

Creek Road

(605) Nettle Creek Road
to Irish Gap

Irish Creek

Irish Creek

NATIONAL

(608) South River Road

South River

Irish Creek Road (603)

to
Lexington

Tour 3

Irish Creek

many privately owned inholdings. More than 42,000 of the forest's million acres lie within Rockbridge County, and they contain a wealth of hiking and jeep trails, fishing streams, campsites, and old mines and quarries. Visit a Forest Service office (see Directory) for maps and information.

In about a mile you'll see the road to the **Tye River Gap Recreation Area** on the right. Another mile brings you to the entrance, on the right, to **Sugar Tree Lodge**.

Several early-19th century Virginia log buildings were moved here, reconstructed, and furnished with antiques to create this unusual country inn.

Another mile and you'll pass under the **Blue Ridge Parkway**.

You could abandon the Tye River Turnpike at this point for the parkway's easier driving and many charms, including the nearby Whetstone Ridge restaurant and gas station (see Tour 18). But you are only a mile and a third from your goal—Irish Creek Road, and the turnpike does become less harrowing from here.

Continue on the turnpike past the Rockbridge/Nelson county line.

Congratulations—you have just crossed the Blue Ridge Divide at an elevation of 2,986 feet. Streams here flow down the east-facing slopes, and the road heads downhill more often than up.

In a mile or so, watch carefully on the right for the junction with Irish Creek Road (603).

Or continue on the turnpike for another mile and a half to Montebello, with its grocery store and restaurant, a modest fishing/camping resort, and a state fish hatchery. Three and a half miles beyond Montebello, the Tye River descends in a long series of rocky cascades called Crabtree Falls. To continue this tour, backtrack on the turnpike to Irish Creek Road.

Just a little way down on the right is Whetstone Ridge Circle (813), an access road to the Whetstone Ridge facilities on the Blue Ridge Parkway.

Irish Creek is a good road, mostly hard-surfaced. The driving is easy and pleasant, gently downhill almost its whole length, as the road descends 1,800 feet to the mouth of Irish Creek. On your right is Whetstone Ridge (2,875 feet); on the left, Painter Mountain (3,305 feet) and then Nettle Mountain (3,330 feet).

This area remained remote and unpeopled, the haunt of panthers and wolves, long after the rest of the country was generally settled. By the 1880s, however, lumbering, quarrying, and mining (and, some say, moonshining) operations were in full swing here. But not for long. No trace now remains of the logging railroads that once climbed the slopes (a spur and trestle have been reconstructed along Blue Ridge Parkway; see page 119). Now the silence is broken only by birdsong and creek babble. Some areas along the road are posted against trespassing, but there are lots of places where you can stop to sit on a rock awhile with your toes in the chilly stream.

In less than a mile from the turnpike you'll pass beneath the Blue Ridge Parkway. Just beyond is the **Grant Cemetery**, which dates from 1851. You are now back in Rockbridge County.

Six miles farther along you'll meet Nettle Creek Road (605), an old road that follows Nettle Creek to cross the Blue Ridge via Irish Gap.

The road leads to the Irish Gap Inns, an elegant

bed-and-breakfast establishment. Watch for a sign saying Private Road near the Blue Ridge Parkway.

The peak now visible on your right is **South Mountain** (2,710 feet), the twin of North Mountain on the other side of the county. As you continue your drive, watch for some unusual rock walls bound with what looks like heavy duty chicken wire.

These walls were built after a devastating flood in 1969 to prevent further erosion of the riverbanks.

Another eight miles of pleasant, winding road brings you to the end of Irish Creek Road at South River Road (608).

This is also the end of Irish Creek, which here empties into the South River. In about 1892 a resort hotel was built at this intersection in anticipation of the development of the mining industry. Economic depression shut down the tin mines just as the hotel was finished; it never opened. A few years later it was dismantled and the materials sold for other projects.

At South River Road you have the options of turning right to return to Vesuvius (about 9 miles) or left to Lexington via Old Buena Vista Road (about 7 miles). Tour 2 describes the South River and Old Buena Vista Roads; you'll find this junction on page 11.

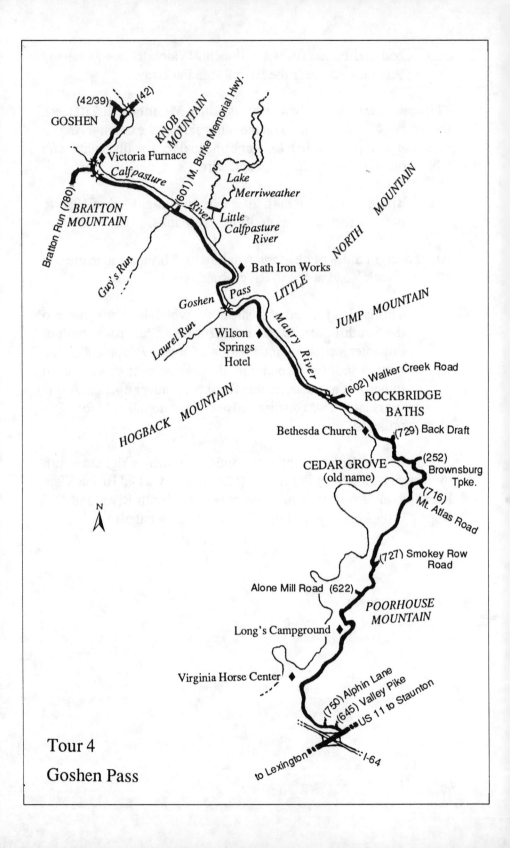

Tour 4

Goshen Pass

Lexington to Goshen:20 miles

The Maury River Road (VA 39) follows the Maury River to the northwest corner of Rockbridge County. The Virginia Horse Center and the village of Rockbridge Baths are along the route; the rocky slopes of dramatic Goshen Pass, topped with stands of pine and softened by rhododendrons, give access to the tiny town of Goshen in the part of the county known as The Pastures. The Maury River Road is designated a Virginia Byway (see page 69), and between Lee Highway (US 11) and Brownsburg Turnpike (VA 252) it is part of the national bicentennial bicycle route.

There are gas stations and convenience stores on Lee Highway near Lexington, along Maury River Road near Rockbridge Baths, and in Goshen. The Virginia Department of Transportation maintains a pleasant wayside in Goshen Pass; it is a popular swimming and fishing spot, with picnic tables, drinking water, and restrooms. Hiking and hunter access trails to the nearby wildlife management areas begin at several spots in and near the pass.

FROM LEXINGTON, go north on Main Street to the junction of Maury River Road and Lee Highway, just north of the I-64 overpass, and turn left; the Super-8 Motel is on the corner. Maury River Road heads west, briefly paralleling I-64, and offers a sweeping view across the valley to House Mountain. It curves north, passing the **Art Farm** (which features a display of classical Chinese painting) and the **Fassifern** bed-and-breakfast inn (on the left), and the

Virginia Horse Center.

The horse center is a first-rate facility for horse breeders and exhibitors in a wide variety of equestrian events. From the road you can see the barns and part of the show rings and pavilions; a fine cross-country course meanders over the rolling hills and through the woods.

Long's Campground is about two miles past the horse center. Beyond Long's, the road twists and climbs for about four and one-half miles as it skirts **Poorhouse Mountain** (1,620 feet), where the county once maintained a farm for the indigent, to the junction with Brownsburg Road (VA 252), once the site of a thriving commercial center. [This junction is the start of Tour 5.]

The settlement of **Cedar Grove**, high on a cliff over the Maury River, was at its peak in the mid-1800s. It boasted two general stores, a blacksmith shop, a post office, a flour mill, and several houses. Grain, whiskey, and pig iron (brought by wagon from the plants at Goshen and Rockbridge Baths) were shipped to Lynchburg or Richmond by narrow wooden batteaux built at nearby boatyards. The boats usually were broken up and sold for firewood at their destination; the crew walked home rather than attempt to pole the 60-foot boats upstream. When the iron industry flagged after the Civil War, Cedar Grove (later called Flumen), also declined. Today there is no sign of the village that aspired to be a metropolis.

A mile and a half beyond Cedar Grove, the **Bethesda Presbyterian Church** perches on a little knoll on the left, its face to the road and its back to the river.

The present brick church was built in 1876, replacing an earlier wooden building; in 1908 the Italianate bell tower was added and a slave gallery was removed. At the same time, a round stained glass window from the Tiffany

Company was installed behind the sanctuary; two other windows may also be Tiffany's work.

Maury River Road crosses Hays Creek just past the church, at the edge of **Rockbridge Baths**, a village out of the 19th century.

The warm springs that once drew health-conscious vacationers to Rockbridge Baths in the late 1800s and early 1900s are hidden behind a low cinder block structure on your right, just beyond the creek; they are not open to the public. The village, formerly known as Jordan's Springs, got its present name in 1857 when a group of investors decided to develop a resort complex, which eventually boasted a luxury hotel and other amenities. General and Mrs. Robert E. Lee were frequent visitors. The hotel burned down in 1926.

Just past the post office (on the left), a swinging footbridge across the Maury provides access for cross-stream residents.

Maury River Road crosses the Maury River, then runs through a relatively flat valley that narrows as it nears **Hogback Mountain** (2,542 feet) to the left and **Jump Mountain** (3,149 feet) to the right. A scant mile and a half past the bridge, on the left, a white, double-galleried private residence stands well back from the road.

It was built in 1775 as the **Wilson Springs Hotel**. The resort was located on the far western boundary of the original Borden grant (described in the introduction). The sulphur springs that prompted development of a vacation spot here are located on an island in the river. At one time there were 20 or 30 cabins nearby, built during the Civil War to house the Confederate soldiers who guarded the pass. In quieter times county families enjoyed a few weeks' respite in late July and early August. The owner, William A. Wilson II, granted a free right to build a cabin on his land to almost anyone who asked. Families with no cabin stayed in the hotel or camped on the floodplain.

Not far beyond the hotel a sign warns of a winding road and a 25-mph speed limit for the three-mile trip through **Goshen Pass**, a rugged and wildly beautiful setting.

There are several places to pull off the road as you drive through the pass. The curves restrict visibility, so be alert for vehicles slowing or entering the highway.

The Maury River splashes boldly in the shallows, forms strong sluices as it forces its way among huge boulders and swirls in swimming pools with colorful local names: Indian, Snake, and Blue Holes, and Devil's Kitchen. The river's narrow banks and the steep, rocky slopes above them are thick with trees and brush. A footpath at **Laurel Run** (on the left) will take you up the mountainside, an especially lovely climb when the rhododendrons blaze with color for a few weeks in the spring.

In the flood of 1985 the river roared. With incredible power it scoured out parts of its channel and altered its course. The pass was closed for nearly two years while the road was rebuilt.

Once called Dunlap's Gap and then Strickler's Pass, it eventually took the name Goshen from the nearby town. Goshen was the nearest rail connection to Lexington, and stagecoaches used this route to connect the little college town to the outside world.

It was by stagecoach that Commodore Matthew Fontaine Maury (1806-1873), for whom the river is named, first viewed Goshen Pass as he arrived to take up his last post, that of Professor of Meteorology at the Virginia Military Institute. A man of many skills, Maury charted trade winds and ocean currents and was instrumental in the successful laying of the Atlantic cable; he was a tactician who aided the Confederacy with coastal defense instruction; he took an LL.D at Cambridge (England); and he was largely responsible for the development of the United States weather bureau. Maury was so taken with the splendor of the pass that he requested his body be carried through there to its final resting place when the rhododendrons were in bloom.

Half a mile beyond the picnic area, on the left, is a bronze tablet which reads:

MAURY—PATHFINDER OF THE SEAS

The genius who first snatched from the ocean and atmosphere the secret of their laws. Born January 14, 1806, died at Lexington, Virginia, February 1, 1873. Carried through Goshen Pass to his last resting place in Richmond, Virginia. Every Mariner for countless ages, as he takes his chart to shape his course across the Seas, will think of thee. His inspiration, Holy Writ—Psalms 8 and 107, Verses 8-23-24; Ecclesiastes 1-8. A tribute to his native State, Virginia, 1923.

A monument to Maury stands across the road.

The ruins of the abandoned **Bath Iron Works** near the west end of the pass are difficult to see without leaving your vehicle.

The brick remains are about 150 yards from the highway, on the right, near the river, and are easiest to spot in winter, when leaves do not obscure the view. Bath was built in 1820 by John Jordan (for whom Jordan's Springs was named) and was one of the busiest foundries in the county.

Once through the tortuous pass, Maury River Road again runs relatively straight, following the **Calfpasture River,** the main tributary of the Maury.

Girl Scout and Boy Scout camps dot the woods across the river. There are a number of popular hiking trails both on **Little North Mountain** (3,070 feet) to the northeast (now behind you) and **Knob Mountain** (2,600 feet), which you can see ahead, on the right.

Between the two mountains (not within sight of the road) is Lake Merriweather, formed by damming another tributary of the Maury, the Little Calfpasture River. The Boy Scout Council of Washington, DC, owns the lake and about 4,000 acres of land. The Goshen Wildlife Management Area lies to the south (on your left), the Little North Mountain Wildlife Management Area to the northeast.

On the right, note the junction with Millard Burke Memorial Highway (601), but don't turn onto it. Its name honors the founder of the Goshen First Aid Crew.

From here Maury River Road runs beside the Calfpasture River between **Bratton Mountain** (3,138 feet) and Knob Mountain for about two miles. It passes a sawmill and the junction with Bratton's Run Road (780), both on the left, then curves to the right.

Just a few hundred feet past the curve, in an open field on the right, are the hulking brick remains of the **Victoria Furnace,** another of the charcoal-fed furnaces that produced much of the iron used by the Confederacy during the Civil War.

Continue on Maury River Road into the **Town of Goshen.**

Goshen Farm gave its name to the Chesapeake & Ohio Railroad station located on its land; the station gave its name to the town that grew up around it. Because The Pastures (as this area is called) is so remote, separated from the rest of Rockbridge County by a range of mountains easily breached only at Goshen Pass, there was a proposal in 1873 to make Goshen the seat of a new county; nothing ever came of it. In the 1890s the town shared the same boom-to-bust cycle experienced by other county towns.

Follow Maury River Road over the CSX railroad tracks (do not turn left onto Alt. 39), past the Cozy Corner Restaurant (on the left) and the Stillwater Worsted Mills (on the right). Where Maury River Road bears left, go straight for a brief but interesting tour beyond **Goshen Bridge.**

> This Registered Virginia Landmark, built in 1890 by Croton Bridge & Manufacturing Company (Croton, New York), is a one-lane, Pratt-type (truss) bridge spanning the Calfpasture River. It is the oldest surviving bridge of its type in the county.

At the end of the road (about half a mile) is **Cameron Hall**, a brick manor house built around 1800 by George Washington Bell.

> Its hipped roof is typical of the then-popular Federal Style. During the boom it served as a resort hotel; it is again a private residence.

Go back across Goshen Bridge and turn right. Follow Maury River Road beside the river as it passes under the CSX railroad bridge and climbs to the stop sign at VA 42. Turn left onto 42 and then left again onto Alt. 39. Continue on Alt. 39 as it passes through the little town center, crosses a couple of sets of railroad tracks, and then meets Maury River Road back at the Cozy Corner Restaurant.

This trip ends here. If you don't want to retrace your route through the pass, take Bratton's Run Road, (near the sawmill) for about eight and a half miles through sparsely populated, densely wooded hollows to Midland Trail (850). Then follow the signs to I-64 east for a quick trip to Lexington, or see Tour 17 for a more leisurely return.

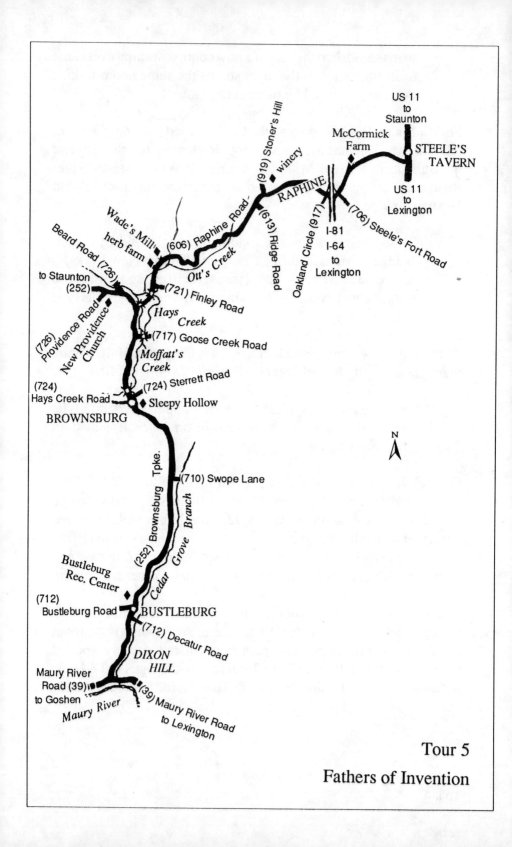

US 11
to
Staunton

McCormick
Farm

STEELE'S
TAVERN

US 11
to
Lexington

(919) Stoner's Hill

winery

RAPHINE

(606) Raphine Road

(613) Ridge Road

Oakland Circle (917)

I-81
I-64
to
Lexington

(706) Steele's Fort Road

Wade's Mill
herb farm

Beard Road (726)

to Staunton
(252)

Ott's Creek

(721) Finley Road

(726) Providence Road

New Providence Church

Hays
Creek

(717) Goose Creek Road

Moffatt's
Creek

(724)
Hays Creek Road

(724) Sterrett Road

Sleepy Hollow

BROWNSBURG

(252) Brownsburg Tpke.

(710) Swope Lane

Cedar Grove Branch

Bustleburg
Rec. Center

(712)
Bustleburg Road

BUSTLEBURG

(712) Decatur Road

DIXON
HILL

Maury River
Road (39)
to Goshen

(39) Maury River Road
to Lexington

Maury River

N

Tour 5

Fathers of Invention

Cedar Grove to Steele's Tavern: 22 miles

A well-maintained two-lane highway, Brownsburg Turnpike (252) climbs away from the Maury River and wends its way through little villages and open farmland. It was not built for speed, but its curves and hills are not difficult if you take your time. Set your mind-clock back to the early 1800s, when grain was harvested by hand and this journey would have been made by horse and wagon.

This tour takes you through Bustleburg, Brownsburg, and Raphine, offers stops at the Buffalo Springs Herb Farm, Wade's Mill, the Rockbridge Vineyard, and the McCormick Farm (a pleasant picnic site), and ends at Steele's Tavern. It is part of a bicentennial bicycle route.

BEGIN THIS TRIP eight and a half miles northwest of Lexington, at the intersection of Maury River Road and Brownsburg Turnpike. To get there, take Lee Highway north to Maury River Road (just north of I-64); follow it for seven and a half miles to Brownsburg Turnpike. See Tour 4 for highlights.

Turn right onto Brownsburg Turnpike. **Dixon Hill** rises to the east as the road climbs away from the Maury River toward the community of **Bustleburg,** about one mile north.

> Local folk will tell you that the town was named when a very fashionable lady lost her composure attempting to ride a horse while wearing a bustle. The Bustleburg Horse Show

is a special local event.

The Bustleburg Recreation Center and ball park, built and maintained by descendants of Ollie T. Wade (1882-1961), who operated a store here, testify to the sense of community that is still important in this part of Virginia. Family-oriented activities such as cake-walks, carnivals, and ham-and-oyster dinners typify weekend possibilities all over the county. These activities are frequently fund-raisers for life-saving crews, volunteer fire departments, families in need, or church and youth groups.

It is four miles from Bustleburg to **Brownsburg.**

The Brownsburg Turnpike connects a number of large farms and smaller holdings that dot the gently rolling valley floor. With the Blue Ridge far to the east and Hogback, Jump, and Little North mountains far to the west, this part of the county has an air of spaciousness about it.

Beyond the junction with Swope Lane (710), a half-mile of maples and oaks show off their vibrant colors in the autumn.

Brownsburg was designated an historic district by the Virginia Historic Landmarks Commission primarily because it has remained nearly unchanged for more than a hundred years. The town was established in 1783 and named for the Reverend John Brown, first pastor of the New Providence Presbyterian Church (page 32). The original plat indicated a main road and two parallel back streets. Stillhouse Alley (named for a distillery at its lower end) and Schoolhouse Alley were the cross streets.

The schoolhouse referred to was the Brownsburg Academy (1848), a Presbyterian high school that once stood atop the hill, behind today's middle school. The academy's bell, cast in Richmond around 1800, is displayed on the main street, in front of the frame building that local folk call the pool hall—reference to a former use.

A visit to the town in 1835 would have revealed a major commercial center with three general stores, two cobblers, three wheelwrights, two blacksmiths, two tailors, a cabinetmaker, carpenter, and hatter. There also were a tavern, tanyard, saddlery, gristmill and mercantile flour mill, and about 20 houses. The saddler was W.R. Wilburn, designer of the Wilburn saddle, noted for its quality and comfort; some of its features appear in today's endurance saddles.

Commerce moved east with the arrival of the railroads, and Brownsburg became the residential community you see today. Craftsman-style architectural detail appears on some of the buildings. Several houses hide log walls beneath weatherboard exteriors; a few buildings have been restored by their owners and others are in the process. Except for a couple of antique shops and the tiny blue post office, all are private homes.

As you pass through town, you can almost hear the tapping hammer of a cobbler at work in the tiny shop behind the house on the corner of Stillhouse Alley ... the quiet singing of slaves in transit, held overnight in the back part of the house on Schoolhouse Alley ... the raucous laughter coming from the house with undressed pine porch posts—a tavern that became a religious meeting room when the building changed owners.

A little side trip to the east on Sterrett Road (724) will reward you with a look at a Sears Roebuck mail-order house.

The first house on the right, a two-story white frame building, is one of the kit houses that Sears sold from its catalog in the 1920s. All the materials were pre-cut and ready to be assembled at the site. These houses are now collectors' items.

The large stone house just beyond is **Sleepy Hollow**, built in 1775. The historic district ends just past Sleepy Hollow.

Return to Brownsburg Turnpike and continue north, following Moffatt's Creek, to visit historic **New Providence Presbyterian Church;** it is a Registered Virginia Landmark.

The congregation was organized in 1746 and occupied two log buildings, a stone building, and a smaller brick structure prior to this Greek Revival Style brick edifice, erected in 1859. Its cemetery (in use since the 1770s) includes the grave of Mary Moore, who was captured by Indians in a raid on Abb's Valley (in Tazewell County, Virginia), and whose family history is entwined with that of this church. One of Mary Moore's direct descendants owns the nearby family farm; it has been in the Moore family for more than 200 years.

Just outside the cemetery is the grave of Sam Houston's brother. It seems he died by leaping from a stagecoach, and as a suicide was denied burial in consecrated ground. Church historians recently determined that the gravesite was unwittingly paved over when the driveway was put in.

The large sycamore tree in front of the church is thought to be the same age as the earlier stone sanctuary, built in 1756. Sycamores are usually found in the bottomland. Local legend says that the seed came from the South River. The girls and women of the congregation rode on horseback between the river and the site, the sand needed for construction in their saddlebags, and the seed hitched a ride.

To continue this trip, backtrack about three-quarters of a mile to the junction with Raphine Road (606), and head east, toward Raphine.

In about a third of a mile, the road crosses Hays Creek where it meets Moffatt's Creek, which drains from the north, and Ott's Creek, which drains from the northeast. Raphine Road follows Ott's Creek upstream for about a half mile to the **Buffalo Springs Herb Farm** and **Wade's Mill.**

The herb farm offers gardens, a plant house, nature trail and picnic area free to visitors and operates a retail herb shop from April to December, but is not open every day. Call for the current schedule (703) 348-1083.

The adjacent Wade's Mill was built in 1750, renovated in 1990, and today supplies bakeries, caterers and folks like you with their fine flours. They also operate April through December. Check with them at (703) 348-1400.

The house behind the mill dates from the late 1700s; the front section was added in 1898. The mill is listed on both the Virginia and National Historic Landmark Registers.

The road rises for a couple of miles beyond the mill, then begins a mile-long gradual descent into Raphine.

The road over this hill was one of the first in the county to have a hard surface; it carried considerable wagon traffic between Brownsburg and Raphine as farmers went to pick up fertilizer and other supplies at the railway depot. The terrain alternates open pasture and wooded hillsides, and there are several abandoned log houses near the road.

Just past the junction with Stoner's Hill Road (919) is the **Rockbridge Vineyard.**

The winery is open for tours and tastings of their eight kinds of wine, which range from apple to pinot noir and chardonet. They're also open April through December, but check their schedule at (703) 377-6204.

Beyond the winery, Raphine Road runs past a couple of farms, then curves into the little village of Raphine.

This rural village, a collection of Victorian buildings, was established in 1883 in anticipation of a direct rail connection to Lexington. The town's founder, J.A.E. Gibbs, who invented the chainstitch sewing machine in 1856, derived the town's name from the Greek word *raphes*, a needle. (One of his machines is on display at the Rockbridge Historical Society in Lexington.)

Raphine Road intersects I-81 about half a mile east of the village. There is a restaurant/coffee shop and auto service available near the interchange. About three quarters of a mile beyond I-81, on the left, is the **McCormick Farm.**

Cyrus Hall McCormick, inventor of the mechanical reaper, was born here in 1809. His father's Walnut Grove Farm is now a National Historic Landmark owned and operated as an agricultural research center by the Virginia Polytechnic Institute. Admission is free.

Robert McCormick, Cyrus's father, experimented with grain-harvesting machinery, but it was his 22-year-old son who made the horse-drawn reaper viable in 1831. The farm's blacksmith shop and gristmill have been faithfully restored. Some beautifully crafted scale models of the reaper in its various stages of evolution are on display, along with photographys of the early machines in action.

There are a few picnic tables. Restrooms are located in a log cabin that was once slave quarters. **Walnut Grove,** the brick manor house built by Robert McCormick about 1823, is used for offices and is not open to the public.

The McCormick Farm straddles the Augusta/Rockbridge county line. From the farm to the junction with Lee Highway in **Steele's**

Tavern, where this trip ends, is about one mile. See page 7 for information about Steele's Tavern.

To return to Lexington, turn right onto Lee Highway (Tour 1, about 16 miles). To return to Lexington via I-81, backtrack on Raphine Road.

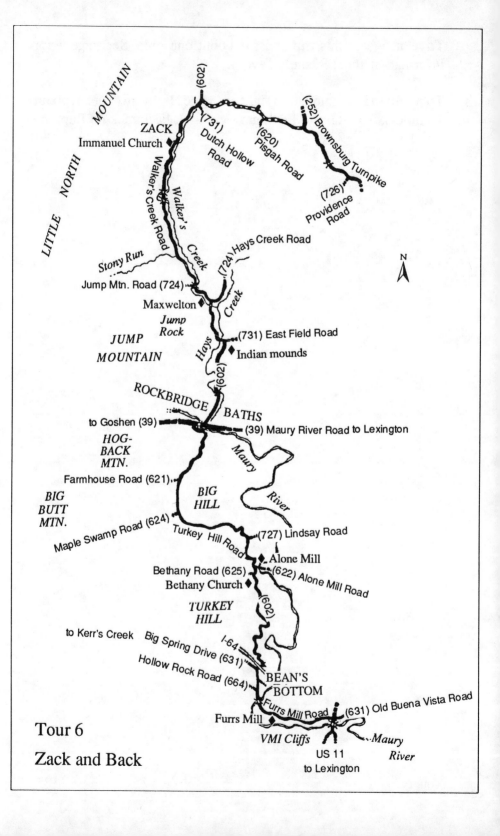

LITTLE NORTH MOUNTAIN

(609)

ZACK
Immanuel Church ◆

(731) Dutch Hollow Road

(620) Pisgah Road

(252) Brownsburg Turnpike

(726) Providence Road

Walker's Creek Road

Walker's Creek

(724) Hays Creek Road

Stony Run

Jump Mtn. Road (724)

Maxwelton ◆

Jump Rock

JUMP MOUNTAIN

Hays Creek

(731) East Field Road

◆ Indian mounds

(602)

ROCKBRIDGE BATHS

to Goshen (39)

(39) Maury River Road to Lexington

HOG-BACK MTN.

Farmhouse Road (621)

Maury River

BIG BUTT MTN.

BIG HILL

Maple Swamp Road (624)

Turkey Hill Road

(727) Lindsay Road

◆ Alone Mill

Bethany Road (625)

Bethany Church ◆

(622) Alone Mill Road

(602)

TURKEY HILL

to Kerr's Creek   Big Spring Drive (631)

I-64

Hollow Rock Road (664)

BEAN'S BOTTOM

Furrs Mill Road   (631) Old Buena Vista Road

Furrs Mill ◆

VMI Cliffs

Maury River

US 11 to Lexington

Tour 6

Zack and Back

N

From Lexington to Zack: 22 miles

This journey mixes old and new as it crosses rivers and hills, skirts mountains, and wends ever northward to the county line. One of the longer tours presented in this book, the round trip from Lexington is about 45 miles.

FROM LEXINGTON, take Main Street north and cross the bridge over the Maury River. Turn left at the traffic light onto Furrs Mill Road (631), which follows the river.

> On the opposite bank is **VMI Island.** Industrial buildings crowded it in the 1800s, when it was called Jordan's Point; now it is the head of the **Chessie Trail,** a seven-mile footpath that follows the abandoned railbed of the C&O Railroad to Buena Vista. The dam and the sewage treatment plant are visible from the road.

About a half mile upstream is the junction with Greenhouse Road (681); bear left as Furrs Mill Road passes the **Lexington Flea Market** and continues on into the floodplain.

> The Virginia Military Institute stands high atop the bluffs across the river; its buildings cannot be seen from here. The sheer cliffs are a rugged backdrop to the deceptively placid river. The wide floodplain and the houses built on stilts attest to periodic flooding.

Just ahead, the road curves to the right to skirt **Furrs Mill.**

Alfred Leyburn built the mill in 1830 and ground grist here until 1901, when D.D. Furr bought it. Burrs for making flour were added about 1924. The three-story frame building was in use until 1962—that's 132 years of service.

Between the mill and a broad cement bridge across the Maury River, look for the familiar silhouette of **House Mountain.** Beyond the bridge lie some of the stoniest fields in the county. On the right is the modern-day community of **Bean's Bottom.** The road parallels I-64 along here. Turn right at Turkey Hill Road (602) to go under the interstate.

Kerr's Creek splashes boldly below a bridge erected in 1992. Just across the bridge, on the right, is a log cabin that was rebuilt from original materials in the late 1980s. The road climbs past a second log house perched above the creek. Both are on private property; please look and take photos from the road.

The road winds and climbs steadily up **Turkey Hill** (1,583 feet). Beyond the hill, **Hogback Mountain's** unmistakable double-humped profile (2,542 feet) rises to the north-northwest.

You'll known you're on Turkey Hill when you see the big stone turkeys perched on a pair of gateposts.

About a mile farther on are the Alone Community Cemetery on the right and **Bethany Evangelical Lutheran Church** on the left.

The congregation was organized in 1859. This small brick church in the Gothic Revival Style was erected in 1904, their second building.

A half mile along the road dips to cross **Alone Mill Creek.**

Snuggled into this cozy hollow, near the spot where Alone Mill Creek empties into the Maury, a mid-19th century Classical Revival brick house and a scattering of other buildings remind visitors of the acitivity that surrounded the once-flourishing mill. The house is well back from the road, on the right, and may be difficult to see in summer; look for the white fence.

In the mile or so beyond Alone Mill, the road climbs again—both in distance and in time—gaining 200 feet of elevation a nd 125 years of industrial progress as it passes beside the power station and under the lines carrying electricity to county residents.

Here, where the road runs east-west, look to the south for a clear view of the twin peaks of **House Mountain**—Little House (3,386 feet) and Big House (3,645 feet)—and the saddle between them.

This part of the county, known as The Barrens in reference to the predominance of pines and open land, recalls the British heritage of some early settlers. Real estate in England was described as either fruiting or barren, depending upon the amount of mast produced for foraging hogs. A stand of oaks provided tasty acorn-fed pork; hogs in a piney wood went hungry.

About two miles beyond the power station, where Turkey Hill Road is again running north-south, pause at the junction with Maple Swamp Road (624) to reorient yourself.

Look for a fire tower on a mountain peak to the west; that's **Big Butt Mountain** (3,451 feet), which lies just this side of Hogback. Rising above the road, to your right, is **Big Hill** (1,700 feet). For the sake of comparison, you are at about 1, 350 feet above sea level.

Maple Swamp Road takes its name from its tendency to go

under water near this junction in wet periods.

Continue on Turkey Hill Road as it wends its way through gently rolling farmland. When you approach the town of **Rockbridge Baths** (described on page 23), the road parallels the river. Turn right to cross the bridge over the Maury River.

Turn right, onto Maury River Road (VA 39), and then left to continue north on Walker's Creek Road (602), which here follows **Hays Creek.** You are now halfway to Zack.

As the road climbs gently, **Jump Mountain** is to the west; the northernmost pinnacle is **Jump Rock** (3,149 feet). A local legend tells of a distraught Indian maiden who, seeing her warrior brave fall in battle, took her own life by throwing herself from this rock. Another version has the young lovers leaping hand-in-hand. You can get a good view of Jump Rock from the entrance road of the Massowomie Program Center, a Girl Scout facility on your left.

Hays Creek carries the name of an early Rockbridge family.

Continue on to the junction with East Field Road (731), where Hays Creek meets **Walker's Creek,** about three-quarters of a mile north.

The Indian battle may be a myth, but there was a prehistoric burial mound here. In 1901, archaeologists from the Valentine Museum in Richmond excavated skeletons of 376 people and eight dogs, along with various artifacts. No evidence of the mound now remains.

About a half mile up the mountain from here, the grave of John Hayes, a major in Daniel Morgan's Revolutionary forces, is marked by a stone cairn and a DAR plaque. Hayes, for whom the creek is named, asked that his body be buried there, overlooking the Indian burial ground. He wanted to be in a good position to see what spirits will arise from the spot when Armageddon comes.

Bear left as Walker's Creek Road follows its namesake. At the junction with Hays Creek Road (724), about a mile and a half north, is **Maxwelton.**

> This 1815 brick manor house stands at the foot of Jump Mountain. Built by Hugh Stuart, the elegant residence sports a two-story Classic Style portico with brick pillars. A summer camp has operated here since 1953. Visitors are welcome.

Bear left on Walker's Creek Road. At the intersection with Jump Mountain Road (724), a picturesque log house perches on a knoll. Turn right, following Walker's Creek Road northward.

> Filling the western horizon, the wall of **Little North Mountain** dominates the lonely landscape, its rippling, pie-crust ridge reaching heights of more than 3,000 feet. Early travelers must have gazed nervously at those thickly forested heights, wondering about bears and panthers and hostile Indians. The ridge is part of the long (twenty miles), narrow Little North Mountain Wildlife Management Area (WMA) of the Jefferson National Forest.

The **McCray-Hunter Access Trail** into the WMA is on the left, a couple of miles beyond the log house.

> A rough road follows Stony Run for a scant half mile and ends at a parking area. The trail and parking area are intended for hunters; there are no picnic facilities or other amenities. But this is an idyllic spot for other visitors to sit for awhile on a mossy rock beside the little creek.

The community of **Zack** is about a mile and half away.

Its post office, no longer open, was named in honor of President Zachary Taylor, who was in office when local postal service was established.

Immanuel Presbyterian Church (founded in 1879) sits beside the road. The wooden church, built in 1904, displays a charming Craftsman-Gothic tower. Its adjoining cemetery includes the tombstone of a woman who died in 1904 at age thirty-one. Her epitaph is lovely:

> She sleeps beneath her native earth,
> And near the spot that gave her birth,
> Her youthful feet trod flowers that bloom,
> In beauty, o'er her early tomb.

This is the end of the trip; Zack is only a mile or so from the Augusta County line. For the return to Lexington, either

Retrace Walker's Creek Road to Rockbridge Baths and follow the Maury River Road (See Tour 4);

Or go a little beyond Zack to High Rock Road (725); bear to the left where the road divides. High Rock is a narrow gravel road that ends at the Brownsburg Turnpike (252) in three miles. A right turn onto the Brownsburg Turnpike will take you to Brownsburg (Tour 5, about two and one-half miles); then follow the signs to I-81. This way will be the faster.

Midland Trail to the Blue Ridge: 19 miles

US 60, known in Rockbridge County as the Midland Trail, in Lexington as Nelson Street, and in Buena Vista as 29th Street, stretches from the Atlantic shore into West Virginia and beyond. In western Virginia it follows the old Midland Trail that brought settlers from Richmond across the Blue Ridge to the frontier. In this excursion, you will be traveling from west to east—from the Valley of Virginia to the crest of the Blue Ridge, with a side tour of the City of Buena Vista.

FROM LEXINGTON, head east on Nelson Street past a stretch of commercial development and under the Alt. US 11 bypass bridge, where Nelson Street becomes a four-lane divided highway called the Midland Trail. The road sweeps across and between the foothills, and in about two miles you'll pass over I-81. Before you is an everchanging *buena vista* (beautiful view) of the imposing Blue Ridge Mountains. The **Maury River**, curving down from the northwest, parallels the highway on your left.

At three and a half miles, watch for **Ben Salem Wayside**, a pleasant and popular riverbank picnic area maintained by the state highway department. Cross the median and pull into the parking lot, or backtrack a hundred feet to another parking area with an easier path down to the wayside.

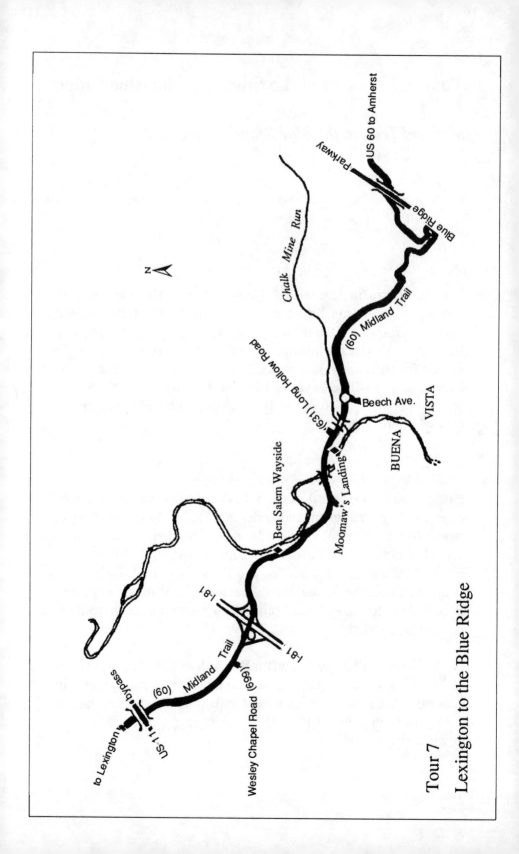

Tour 7
Lexington to the Blue Ridge

Here you will find a remnant of the North River Navigation system: a well-preserved lock, one of nine that permitted canal boats to navigate the Maury (then called North River) between the James River and Lexington in the 1860s and 1870s. There are tree-shaded picnic tables and a few fireplaces. Bird-watching is excellent along the reedy banks.

Across the river you can see the Chessie Nature Trail, a seven-mile-long footpath that follows the former railroad bed between Lexington and Buena Vista. Rail service to Lexington ended in 1969.

Back on the highway, on the right, is a charming coffee-pot shaped building that was a restaurant 30 years ago.

Now it is the headquarters of the **James River Basin Canoe Livery,** where you can rent equipment for all sorts of canoe trips in the region. They also offer classes in basic and whitewater canoeing.

Half a mile farther along, the road crests a hill, then dips to cross the river. [Note, at the top of the hill, the junction with Forge Road (608) (Tour 8) to the right.]

The road narrows to three lanes through a riverside industrial area. On the right, an historical marker recalls **Moomaw's Landing,** part of the old North River Navigation system.

D.C. Moomaw owned a 370-acre estate here, called Green Forest; he established a village and planned a city, but sold out to the Buena Vista Company, formed to promote development of the region's mineral wealth.

US 60, now 29th Street in the city of **Buena Vista,** passes under the Norfolk Southern Railroad bridge and intersects Magnolia Avenue (US 501) at the traffic light.

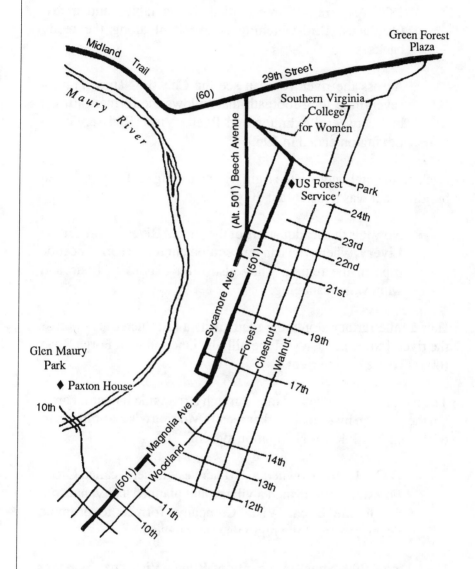

Tour 7
Buena Vista

Turn right on Beech Street, then turn left at the next traffic light, just a short block away. Bear left after the turn and drive up onto the **Southern Virginia College for Women** campus; from there you will have a lovely view of the city and the Blue Ridge.

This part of the county was originally known as Green Forest and Hart's Bottom. The City of Buena Vista took its name from the nearby Buena Vista iron furnace (see page 12). The city was developed in the nationwide post-Civil War boom (1889-1892), with the help of northern capital. Within three years, this once-rural area became a city with 5,240 residents and 22 businesses. The iron industry was the main focus; easy access to the James River for shipping encouraged entrepreneurs to build wagons, make brick and glass, and provide other support for the anticipated growth. By 1893, however, the boom had gone bust.

Many downtown buildings date from the boom, and the Main Hall of Southern Virginia College for Women, the only survivor of several hotels built in the county, is a well-preserved and beautiful example of the period. SVCW, known as Southern Seminary College for Women ("Southern Sem") until a name change in 1993, is a two-year liberal arts college for women. The riding rings attest to a strong interest in horsemanship.

Drive on past Main Hall and turn right onto Chestnut Avenue as you exit the campus. Turn right again onto Park Avenue at the bottom of the hill, then left onto Magnolia Avenue at the stop sign.

The US Forest Service Pedlar District office is on the left side of Magnolia in the first block after you turn. You can stop here for maps, information, and advice about hiking trails, camping, fishing, and hunting in the nearby George Washington National Forest. The office is open on weekdays.

Continue south on Magnolia through Buena Vista's renovated downtown district, a congenial mix of old and new buildings.

> At Magnolia and 21st Street is the Buena Vista branch of the Rockbridge Regional Library. It occupies the building that once housed the headquarters of the Buena Vista Company. The building was renovated in 1989 and now appears as it did nearly a hundred years ago.

Near the south end of town, at 10th Street, turn right to visit **Glen Maury Park.** [Note: to reach the beginning of Tour 9, stay on Magnolia, which will become the Glasgow Highway in another mile or so.]

> Developed in the late 1960s, the 315-acre municipal park across the Maury River has a two-story pavilion, picnic acreas with shelters, a swimming pool, nature trails, and RV and tent camping sites. Elisha Paxton's 1827 house, a Registered Virginia Landmark, overlooks tennis courts and athletic fields and serves as a senior citizen center. Paxton was the head of a large family which is still representeed in the county; the family cemetery is located east of here, on Forge Road (page 52).

When you exit the park, turn left onto 10th Street, then left onto Magnolia. At 17th Street turn right for a block or two, then turn left again to parallel Magnolia.

> Any of the pleasant, tree-lined back streets offers a lovely array of gracious older homes mixed with stately, well kept churches in real hometown-America setting.

At 22nd Street turn left, cross Magnolia, turn right onto Sycamore Avenue, and then immediately bear left onto Beech Avenue.

> Beech has some interesting old commercial buildings.

The **General Store** is a modern-day emporium that offers all of the goods things once found in old-fashioned general stores, including a number of items made in Virginia. Stop for a soft drink and a friendly game of checkers by the wood stove.

At the traffic light near the college note the **Arcade,** a wooden building on the right that is typical of the commercial architecture of the post-Civil War boom. It has recently undergone extensive renovation.

The second traffic light is at the intersection of Beech and 29th Street. Turn right to resume your drive on the old Midland Trail.

At the outskirts of town, beyond the Green Forest Plaza shopping center, the road begins a steep, curving climb (about 1,200 feet in four miles) up the pine-fragrant, rocky slopes of Humphrey's Gap to the **Blue Ridge Parkway.**

The highway is well engineered, but it does require your full attention. (You will see, westbound, an escape lane for runaway trucks.)

The Midland Trail crests the Blue Ridge at milepost 45.6 on the parkway. Following the signs, turn south onto the parkway to a parking area just 500 feet from the entrance. This overlook offers a sweeping view of the territory you have just driven—to Buena Vista and beyond—from 2,325 feet above sea level.

This trip ends here, at the overlook. Retrace the route to return to Lexington, or see Tour 18 for a description of the parkway's many delights and other return options.

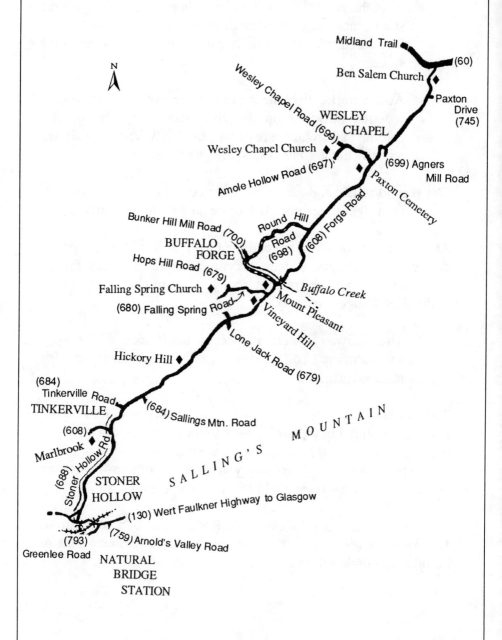

Midland Trail

Ben Salem Church

(60)

Paxton
Drive
(745)

Wesley Chapel Road (699)

WESLEY
CHAPEL

Wesley Chapel Church

Amole Hollow Road (697)

(699) Agners
Mill Road

Paxton Cemetery

Round Hill
Road
(698)

(608) Forge Road

Bunker Hill Mill Road (700)

BUFFALO
FORGE

Hops Hill Road (679)

Falling Spring Church

(680) Falling Spring Road

Buffalo Creek

Mount Pleasant

Vineyard Hill

Lone Jack Road
(679)

Hickory Hill

(684)
Tinkerville Road

TINKERVILLE

(684) Sallings Mtn. Road

(608)

Marlbrook

Stoner Hollow Rd.
(688)

STONER
HOLLOW

SALLING'S   MOUNTAIN

(130) Wert Faulkner Highway to Glasgow

(793)

(759) Arnold's Valley Road

Greenlee Road   NATURAL
BRIDGE
STATION

Tour 8

Buffalo Forge

Ben Salem to Natural Bridge Station: 12 miles

Forge Road (608) runs from the Midland Trail (US 60) southward past rolling farmland, the ghost of an 1800s industrial complex, and some beautiful manor houses. It links the little communities of Wesley Chapel, Falling Spring, Tinkerville, and Natural Bridge Station.

FROM LEXINGTON, take Nelson Street/Midland Trail eastward (toward Buena Vista). This leg of your journey is described in Tour 7. Watch for Forge Road about four miles beyond the US 11 bypass, and turn right. In just two-tenths of a mile, on a little knoll above the road, to the left, is the tiny stone **Ben Salem Presbyterian Church.**

> Ben Salem (Son of Peace) was organized in 1832; the congregation met in a boat shed near the Ben Salem lock on the Maury River. A stone church was built near there, but it suffered damage from frequent flooding. Stones from the original church were used in the construction of this building in 1884. The congregation was dissolved for lack of members around the turn of the century, but was reorganized in 1951. The stained glass windows, designed by a local artist, were added in 1977.

About two miles beyond the church, turn right at the junction with Wesley Chapel Road (699). An easy half-mile side trip will take you through the little community of **Wesley Chapel**, to the **Wesley**

Chapel United Methodist Church.

This simple brick church (1873) sits on a low hill with its cemetery spread like a hoop skirt below it. There is a lovely view of the Blue Ridge from the hilltop.

Return to Forge Road and turn right. A few yards down the road, on a little knoll to the right, is the **Paxton Family Cemetery.** A cement stairway climbs the steep embankment; it may be hidden by vegetation in the summer.

Several generations of the Paxton family who lived and died in this part of the county in the 18th and 19th centuries are buried in this little cemetery. A few of the gravestones are in the shape of a doorway, which symbolizes the soul's passing on to higher realms. Some are elaborately carved on the back. Elisha Paxton's home stands in Glen Maury Park in Buena Vista (see page ##).

About two miles south of the Paxton Cemetery, as the road crests a hill, bear right onto Round Hill Road (698) for a pleasant side trip of about three miles. Round Hill is a narrow gravel road, but it is not difficult to drive. It does, however, cross a low-water bridge; if the creeks are up, stay on Forge Road.

This country road plunges into the rugged wilderness experienced by the Indians and early pioneers. It winds through an untamed rural landscape—tight little fields and dense woods—and ends at a low-water bridge spanning **Buffalo Creek.** Cross the bridge and turn left onto Bunker Hill Mill Road (700) to follow the creek downstream, back to Forge Road. Even at low water the creek runs with the strength of a small river, more than enough to drive the mill that stood near here until the 1960s. There are a few places where the shoulder of the road is wide enough to park your vehicle and listen for awhile to the water music.

Whether you chose to explore on Round Hill Road or continued southward on Forge Road, you will soon reach **Buffalo Forge,** the ghostly remnants of a major industrial complex. This compound is privately owned and not open to the public.

> **Mount Pleasant,** a very large stone house with a red roof and five white gables, was built in the late 18th century by James Beggs. It has been extensively remodelled, but retains its original charm. In summer, the best view from the road is found near the top of the hill.
>
> The time-ravished remains of **Brady's Mill** are below the house, in a hollow. The roof has collapsed; the wheel is gone. In summer, look for the tops of its stone walls in the stand of trees that have grown up along the millrace.
>
> Developed by William Weaver in the mid-1800s, Buffalo Forge was a typical iron plantation with a gristmill, general store, sawmill, smithy, leather shop, carpenter shop, post office, ice house, stables, dairy barn, slave quarters, kitchen, guest cottage, and manor house. The holdings included about 7,200 acres of heavily wooded mountain land. Timber was essential; it was turned into the charcoal used to fuel the furnaces. The water power from Buffalo Creek made this an ideal site for a foundry. Iron was a very marketable commodity both in the growing new nation and in Europe; the lack of timber in England had forced the closure of blast furnaces there.
>
> The Tredegar Iron Works in Richmond accepted most of the pig iron from Rockbridge. During the Civil War, this valley supplied nearly all the iron for the Confederacy—including that used in the armor plates on the USS *Merrimac* (which was re-christened the *Virginia* when the Confederates took her over).

About a third of a mile to the south is the junction with Falling

Spring Road (680). Turn here for a pleasant side trip to **Falling Spring Presbyterian Church** and its cemetery, a scant mile to the west.

> The congregation was organized in a log building about three miles south of here in 1746, moved to a stone church on this site in 1749, and then erected the present brick sanctuary in 1862. The brigade of Confederate troops camped in the field across the road during its dedication must have been an incongruous and unhappy sight in this pastoral setting.
>
> The cemetery has some good examples of doorway-shaped gravestones mentioned above. The oldest honors "Soldier" John Grigsby, patriarch of the populous Grigsby clan. His three-lobed stone (1794) is inscribed:
>
> > Pause Reader, here and look with solemn dread
> > Upon the last lone dwelling of the dead;
> > Tho' num'rous graves appear on every hand,
> > This was the first of all the silent band.
>
> Lambs often appear on the gravestones of children. There is an unusual freestanding stone lamb on the gravestone of Hugh Blair Chandler, an infant who died in 1854.

From Falling Spring Church, return to Forge Road and turn right to continue your journey southward. There is a stone manor house on the right, not far from the junction with Falling Spring Road. Look for a section of split-rail fence at the bottom of the hill; there is room to pull off the road and enjoy the view.

> **Vineyard Hill** (late 18th century) was built by Alexander Beggs, another of the Beggs clan that settled this area prior to the industrial age. The stone house sits on a little knoll halfway up the hillside. Below it are well-kept lawns, a little creek, and various stone walls and buildings.

About a half mile past Vineyard Hill, on the right side of the road, there is first a stretch of timber and then a large pasture fenced with barbed wire. The fence runs to the intersection of Lone Jack Road (679), which can be seen a hundred yards or so ahead. Stop anywhere along here, and look across the rolling pasture for a view of Falling Spring Presbyterian Church nestled against the hillside in the distance.

> The fields in front of the church were a natural choice for an army encampment. If you listen carefully, you may hear the voices of Confederate soldiers calling out to one another from the tree-lined hollows.

Continue south on Forge Road about a mile and a half to **Hickory Hill**, on your right. A roadside sign identifies it.

> One of the Seven Hill homes (see page 64), Hickory Hill was built around 1823-24 by Reuben Grigsby. Although this brick Federal Style house is situated some distance from the road, it can easily be seen—a jewel cast in a fold of green and gold brocade. A broad, two-story porch on a high ground floor gives the effect of a triple portico.

About half a mile beyond Hickory Hill, on the left, you will pass the junction with Salling's Mountain Road (864), the road to Glasgow. For the next half mile, Forge Road skirts the vaguely defined community of **Tinkerville,** once a part of the vast Hickory Hill plantation.

> Tinkerville, once a collection of small shops and homes of carpenters, coopers, farmhands and woocutters that flourished here in the 1880s and 1890s, now provides a quiet setting for a few modern families. The heart of Tinkerville is about a mile or so from here, on Tinkerville Road (684), which bears off to the right.

Don't turn on Tinkerville Road; stay on Forge Road. In another half mile, Forge Road makes a sharp turn to the right and follows a white wooden fence to the entrance of **Marlbrook** (on the left).

> When David Greenlee, Sr., built this simple brick house about 1777, he called it Cherry Hill and planted a cherry orchard to justify its name. It was one of the earliest of the Grigsby-Greenlee Seven Hills homes.

Turn around at the entrance to Marlbrook and go back to the junction with Stoner Hollow Road (688), then turn right.

> This woodsy stretch of road follows **Crawford Creek** as it bubbles cheerfully over the toes of **Salling's Mountain** (ahead of you, then to your left) as you head downstream through **Stoner Hollow**, named for a family that farmed here from about 1890 until the mid 1960s.

In about two miles, beside a sheer limestone wall, the road splits. Take the downhill branch to the left, to pass beneath Wert Faulkner Highway bridge (VA 130). (The right-hand branch climbs to a dangerous junction with the highway.)

The stone Norfolk Southern Railroad culvert is ahead of you. Go under it, then bear left as Lloyd Tolley Road (773) climbs about a quarter of a mile through part of the community of **Natural Bridge Station** to the highway, where this journey ends. (See pages 71-73 for more information about Natural Bridge Station.)

> In the little village center you'll find a restaurant, post office, bank, and a lumberyard. A logging operation, an antique shop, and a country store are nearby.

Turn left (west) and Wert Faulkner Highway will take you to Lee Highway (US 11) at Natural Bridge (see Tours 10 and 11), and back to Lexington. Or turn right (east) on Wert Faulkner Highway and drive about a quarter of a mile to the beginning of Tour 12, a closed loop in and out of Arnold's Valley.

Buena Vista to Balcony Falls: 8 miles

This journey follows the Maury River south from Buena Vista to Glasgow; it skirts the George Washington National Forest and climbs rugged slopes where the James River cuts through the Blue Ridge in a four-mile-long series of cascades known as Balcony Falls.

FROM LEXINGTON, take Nelson Street (US 60) east about six miles to Buena Vista, then take US 501 south about four-and-a-half miles. Beyond the city limits you'll be on Glasgow Highway (Tour 7 describes what you'll see between Lexington and the beginning of this trip.) Look for a narrow road that forms the right-hand fork of a Y—River Road (663)—and turn onto it.

Six and a half miles long, River Road hugs the Maury, and at several points you can see remnants of the 19th-century North River Navigation Company dams and locks. There are no crossroads, nor any way to cross the river. The road rejoins Glasgow Highway just north of Glasgow. The Norfolk Southern railroad tracks follow the river on the opposite bank.

To the east, between the highway and the river, is **Brady Hill** (1,529 feet). The small mountain across the river to the south is **Miller Mountain** (1,686 feet), with the higher **Salling's Mountain** (1,805 feet) behind it. About midway

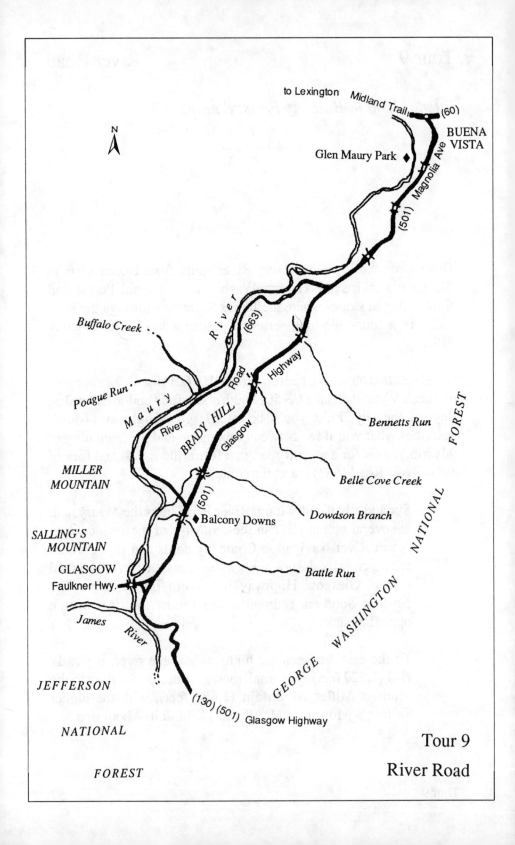

to Lexington Midland Trail

(60)

BUENA
VISTA

Glen Maury Park

Magnolia Ave

(501)

N

River

(663)

Buffalo Creek

Highway

Poague Run

Bennetts Run

Maury

River

Road

BRADY HILL

Glasgow

MILLER
MOUNTAIN

Belle Cove Creek

(501)

Balcony Downs

Dowdson Branch

SALLING'S
MOUNTAIN

GLASGOW
Faulkner Hwy.

Battle Run

James

River

JEFFERSON

WASHINGTON

NATIONAL

FOREST

GEORGE

NATIONAL

(130) (501) Glasgow Highway

FOREST

Tour 9

River Road

on River Road, the Maury is joined by **Buffalo Creek,** which drains much of the southwest quadrant of the county.

At the stop sign (where River Road meets Glasgow Highway) turn right. Just beyond this junction you'll see the sign for the **Balcony Downs** bed-and-breakfast inn.

> This stately, pillared 1802 manor house sits amid fifty acres of the original working plantation at the edge of the George Washington National Forest.

Just beyond the meadows at Balcony Downs the road crosses **Battle Run,** site of the first Indian fight in the county (1742).

> The skirmish involved thirty-three Iroquois Indians and thirty-four white settlers led by Captain James McDowell. The cause of the fight is unclear, but it resulted in the death of 8 settlers (including McDowell) and 17 Indians. (The white casualties of this encounter are buried in the McDowell family cemetery north of Lexington. See page **56.**)
>
> In 1742, various factions claimed jurisdiction in the Valley of Virginia. Although the British Crown was granting settlement rights, the Iroquois Indians claimed certain rights by virtue of treaty. The governor of Pennsylvania mediated the dispute and ruled that the whites were the aggressors. Virginia's Governor Gooch paid the Iroquois £100 in retribution. The Iroquois gave up their rights to the valley when they signed the Treaty of Lancaster (Pennsylvania) two years later.

A mile or so south of Balcony Downs, on the right, are two stone gateposts. The inscription *Willow Grove 1780* alludes to a mansion that no longer exists. Just beyond is the junction with Wert Faulkner Highway to the town of Glasgow (see Tour 11). Stay on Glasgow Highway.

Since the road pulls away from the river, you can't see the confluence of the Maury and the James from here. There is a small turnout on the right, about a half mile from the Faulkner Highway junction, where you can see the two rivers when the trees are not in full leaf.

Glasgow Highway takes advantage of the James River water gap as it cuts through the Blue Ridge. The road is steep, with well-banked curves. Two shady waysides (one with picnic tables, both on the right) about two miles above Glasgow are the best places to view **Balcony Falls.**

> This four-mile stretch of the James River drops 200 feet in a series of turbulent cascades. The *bal-CO-ny*, as it was known to the rivermen, was infamous for its treacherous waters, made so by the narrow channel and immense boulders. Lives and cargo were lost frequently. The opening of the James River Canal in 1850 greatly reduced the risk of shipping by water.
>
> The road, too, was used to transport the products of the county to market. Within the memory of one county resident are annual cattle drives from her father's farm in Natural Bridge Station to Lynchburg. She recalls the year her eight-year-old sister insisted on making the trip—and completed it successfully, sharing a horse part of the way and walking the rest.

End this trip at the second wayside, where markers tell of the establishment of Rockbridge and Amherst counties. (Bedford County, by the way, is just across the river at this point.)

To get back to Lexington, you can

> •retrace your drive on Glasgow Highway;
>
> •take Wert Faulkner Highway to Natural Bridge (Tour 11,

about 21 miles);

•or continue on Glasgow Highway (US 501) a couple of miles to the Blue Ridge Parkway (Tour 18) and take it north to return to Lexington via Buena Vista (Tour 7, about 31 miles).

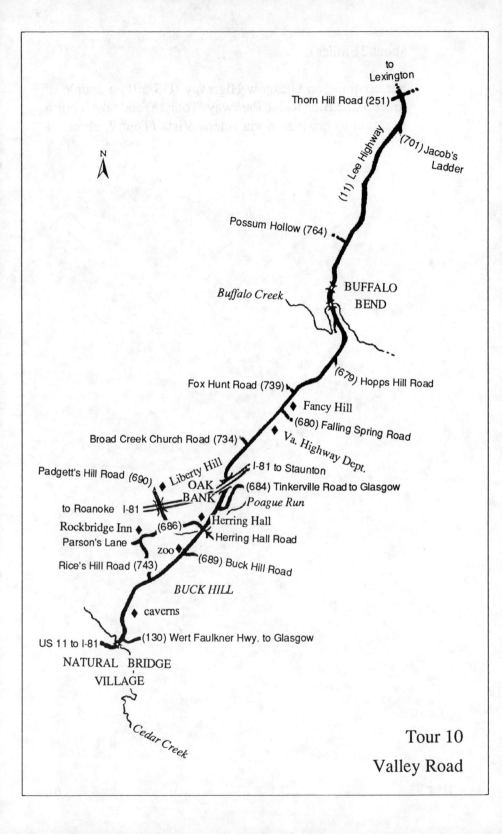

to
Lexington

Thorn Hill Road (251)

(701) Jacob's
Ladder

(11) Lee Highway

Possum Hollow (764)

Buffalo Creek

BUFFALO
BEND

(679) Hopps Hill Road

Fox Hunt Road (739)

♦ Fancy Hill

(680) Falling Spring Road

Broad Creek Church Road (734)

♦ *Va. Highway Dept.*

Padgett's Hill Road (690)   Liberty Hill

I-81 to Staunton

OAK
BANK

(684) Tinkerville Road to Glasgow

to Roanoke I-81

Poague Run

Rockbridge Inn   (686)   Herring Hall

Parson's Lane   ♦   Herring Hall Road

zoo ♦

Rice's Hill Road (743)   (689) Buck Hill Road

BUCK HILL

♦ caverns

US 11 to I-81   (130) Wert Faulkner Hwy. to Glasgow

NATURAL   BRIDGE
VILLAGE

Cedar Creek

Tour 10

Valley Road

Tour 10   Valley Road

Lexington to Natural Bridge: 14 miles

The Robert E. Lee Highway (US 11) is a three-lane, well-graded road. From Lexington southward it offers an easy, pleasant drive through the Valley of Virginia and a variety of sights—from pigmy goats to giant dinosaurs, from tiny cabins to stately manors, from rustic campsites to a deluxe hotel, from deep dark caverns to a soaring stone bridge.

BEGIN THIS TRIP at the traffic light south of Lexington, where Lee Highway (the Alt. US 11 bypass) and Link Road (VA 251) meet. Head south on Lee Highway, toward Natural Bridge.

> The road undulates past farms with steep pastures, the sort of terrain that inspired all the jokes about cows in Appalachia having downhill legs longer than uphill legs so they won't walk at a slant. Redbud trees along here provide a spectacular display in the spring.

Four and a half miles south of Lexington lies **Buffalo Bend,** a small cluster of homes beside the road at **Buffalo Creek.**

> The creek, which drains the southwestern quadrant of the county, curves sharply here as it flows toward the Maury River. The shallow rapids of this broad, clear creek run with a murky intensity when it gathers the runoff of even light rains across the county.

The open, rolling farmland south of Buffalo Bend permits a view to the natural boundaries of the county—the Blue Ridge to the east and the Allegheny Mountains to the west.

About two and a half miles beyond Buffalo Bend, an imposing manor house commands a sweeping view of the valley from its hilltop site. **Fancy Hill** is one of the *Seven Hill* homes.

In the late 1700s and early 1800s the Grigsby and Greenlee families built large homes in this area, each with the word *Hill* in its name, an allusion to the Seven Hills of Rome. *Fruit Hill* (northeast of here) was owned by "Soldier" John Grigsby, a soldier in the Revolutionary War, and Lawrence Washington, brother of our first president. *Rose Hill* (near Buffalo Bend; it cannot be seen from the road) was built by John's son, Elisha Grigsby.

Fancy Hill was owned by Sally Grigsby Welsh, Soldier John's eldest daughter, her husband, Thomas Welsh II, who was her first cousin, and their 14 children. For a time it was used as a stage-coach stop known as Welsh's Tavern. It later housed the Fancy Hill Academy, a boys' school run by David Laird.

Clover Hill, now known as Herring Hall (pages 65-66), was home to Hannah Ingram Grigsby (one of Elisha's daughters), her husband, David Greenlee, and their 12 children. The *Liberty Hill* farm (page 66), which adjoined Clover Hill to the west, was another holding of Sallie and Thomas Welsh II. You will see these two homes a few miles south of here.

Cherry Hill, now called Marlbrook (page 56), and *Hickory Hill* (page 55) can be seen on Forge Road (Tour 8).

Just past Fancy Hill, at Falling Spring Road (680), an historical marker announces **Falling Spring Presbyterian Church,** about two and a half miles away on Forge Road. For information about it, see page 54.

The **Virginia Department of Highways** area office is two-tenths of a mile south of here.

In another mile and a half, just beyond the **KOA Campground** entrance, bear left to pass under the interstate bridges. The road rises; stop near the top of the hill (park at the grocery store, gas station, or restaurant) and look back toward Lexington.

> The view is lovely. Big and Little House mountains rise from the valley floor; weathered barns and tidy farm houses dot the landscape. The cluster of businesses and homes here comprise the community of **Oak Bank.**

Less than half a mile past the interstate is the **Enchanted Castle.**

> A local artist creates fiberglass figures in this exotic studio-cum-amusement park that is sometimes open to the public.

Beyond the Castle, at the bottom of the hill, turn right onto Herring Hall Road (686) to follow a path of history once called the Valley Road.

> Travelers forded Cedar Creek at the nearby Red Mill in the late 18th and early 19th centuries (see page 96), when the Valley Road was a main thoroughfare. The road was used less frequently when traffic began to flow across the Natural Bridge, the route of today's US 11. The little stream near this intersection is **Poague Run.**

On Herring Hall Road, just west of Lee Highway, is **Herring Hall** itself, the youngest of the Seven Hills homes (1832).

> Originally called Clover Hill by its builders, David

Greenlee and Hannah Grigsby, this brick house was known to travelers as Greenlee Tavern. Its strategic location near the bottom of this steep hill assured it of a steady clientele who sought refreshment and rest before returning to the dusty road. The house has unusual oval attic windows.

At the junction with Padgetts Hill Road (690), turn right for a little side trip to **Liberty Hill,** about a half mile from here.

This brick house perches atop the hill to the right, its hilly fields bounded by a white board fence. A sign on the mailbox and another near the gate identify this 1823 Federal Style building.

Return to Herring Hall Road and turn right. The road curves sharply to the left about a mile beyond Herring Hall. The two-story brick house on the curve is the **Rockbridge Inn.**

This inn (built about 1775) has unusual porches that wrap around both the ground floor and upper story. Now a private residence, this house was one of the earliest stage-coach stops on the Valley Road.

Bear left onto Rices Hill Road (743) at the Inn.

Just down the road, on the right, is a renovated two-story cabin built on land once owned by Thomas Jefferson. Did he ever visit the cabin? It is quite possible that he did; the history detectives are still at work on this mystery.

Continue a scant mile to the stop sign at Lee Highway. Turn left to visit the **Natural Bridge Zoo.** (The zoo is open April through November; there is an entrance fee.)

For a change of pace, stroll shoulder to shoulder with a llama or an oryx in their spacious pasture, stare at a bear, ogle the lions and tigers, feed the goats, marvel at the exotic birds and monkeys, and a whole lot more. There are picnic tables in a covered pavilion. Soft drinks are available; bring your own food.

Upon leaving the zoo, turn right onto Lee Highway. A mile to the south are the **Natural Bridge Caverns**.

The caverns reach deep into the earth beneath Buck Hill. Guided tours last forty-five minutes to an hour and are a particular treat in the summer, as the cavern temperature is 54° F. year-round. A light jacket is recommended. There is a gift shop, and you are welcome to picnic at tables on a shaded hillside.

Return to the highway and turn left. Just two-tenths of a mile down the road is the **Natural Bridge Village**.

The complex includes the bridge itself, a wax museum, a gift shop, and a variety of food services (snacks to fine dining). Other amenities, such as a swimming pool and tennis courts, are restricted to guests of the Natural Bridge Hotel. There is an information desk in the gift shop.

The US Forest Service staffs a seasonal information center here, across the road from the large parking lot. The tiny Natural Bridge post office is located beneath the gift shop.

The jewel in this crown is, of course, the **Natural Bridge,** which was surveyed by George Washington and owned by Thomas Jefferson. The path down to the bridge follows a brook that drops in a series of little waterfalls past an ancient *arbor vitae*. There are many steps; a shuttle bus is available if you prefer to ride. A smooth, easy footpath follows Cedar Creek through its deep gorge, passes under the Bridge, detours slightly at an abandoned saltpeter mine, and ends near a lacy waterfall. A sound-and-light show depicting the Drama of Creation is presented nightly.

Jefferson delighted in the bridge and was a frequent visitor. In 1817 he brought his granddaughters, Ellen and Cornelia, with him from his Poplar Forest retreat in Amherst County. The road was too rough for a wagon, so they crossed the Blue Ridge on horseback, a rigorous 29-mile trip through Petite's Gap in Arnold's Valley. Upon their return home, Cornelia reported that the bridge was all their grandfather had promised, but that she and her sister were ill-prepared for the primitive roads, the rough frontier folk they met, and the filthy cabin in which they spent the night. (Current management reports no such complaints!)

The **Natural Bridge Wax Museum** offers a self-guided tour of historical and religious wax figures in animated displays. The fascinating manufacturing process is explained in the Factory Tour, and visitors may have a photo taken with the figure of famous person—Elizabeth Taylor as Cleopatra, General Robert E. Lee, and Elvis Presley were seen there recently.

This trip ends here, in the Natural Bridge Village. If you want to drive across the bridge, take Lee Highway past the main hotel to the top of the hill, where it crosses the ninety-foot-wide chasm on the Natural Bridge—215 feet above Cedar Creek.

To return to Lexington via another route, see the master map inside the front cover.

Tour 11   Down by the Station

Natural Bridge to Glasgow: 6.5 miles

This trip is short in length but long in history. It takes but ten or fifteen minutes to drive from one end to the other, but 250 years to get from John Salling's 1740 land grant to the 1990's Rockbridge Industrial Park, with a pleasant side trip through the Victorian village of Natural Bridge Station.

BEGIN THIS DRIVE at the Natural Bridge Village (Lee Highway, fifteen miles south of Lexington), where Wert Faulkner Highway (VA 130), an official Virginia Byway, skirts Buck Hill behind the wax museum and meanders eastward.

> Roads of unusual natural beauty that give access to spots of particular aesthetic or cultural value are designated as scenic byways by the Commonwealth Transportation Board. Although the commonwealth selects the roads so honored, it is up to the local authorities to ensure that these roads retain their pleasing appearance.

About a mile and a half down the road, just past the **Natural Bridge General Store,** is one of the prettiest waysides in the county. The shady glade with a tiny, gurgling brook is kept fresh and inviting by the Glasgow Garden Club.

In another half mile, on a hill overlooking the road, is the US Forest Service's **Glenwood Ranger Station.**

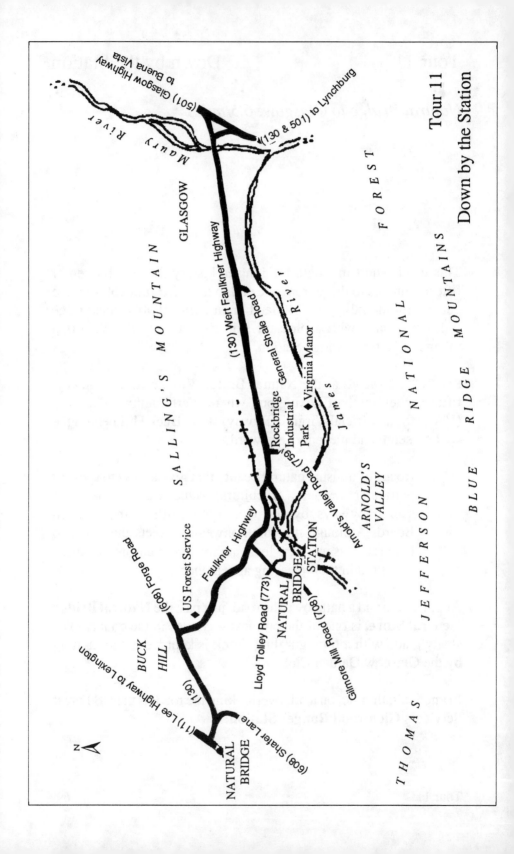

Tour 11

Down by the Station

There are four US Forest Service Districts that administer 63,00 acres within Rockbridge County. Glenwood oversees 20,974 acres of the Jefferson National Forest within the county. Maps, literature, and other information can be obtained here year-round.

The speed limit drops to 40 mph a scant half-mile past the ranger station, your signal to look for the green-and-white sign at Gilmore Mill Road (708) announcing your arrival in **Natural Bridge Station.** Turn right onto Gilmore Mill Road, then stop to enjoy the view.

The Blue Ridge forms an imposing backdrop for a little village that could serve as inspiration for a model railroad layout. Both the Norfolk Southern and the CSX tracks run through here; the NS crosses the broad James River on a sturdy trestle. There are a couple of red brick schools, a bank, a lumberyard with a logging operation behind it, a tiny post office tucked in beside The Corner Grill, a scattering of Victorian houses, antique shops, and a modern industrial park. All this nestles snugly against the slopes of wooded Salling's Mountain.

The village grew up around the Natural Bridge station of the Shenandoah Valley Railroad (now the Norfolk Southern). Day-trippers from Richmond and Lynchburg were shuttled between the station and the Natural Bridge in horse-drawn buggies. Folks from the humid tidewater regions delighted in the temperate mountain climate.

To explore the village a little, continue on Gilmore Mill Road a few hundred yards and turn left at Lloyd Tolley Road (773).

The road climbs here for a nice view of the James River and the Norfolk Southern trestle that spans it, then swings downhill to the left, into what used to be the station area. The station no longer exists, but there are a few commercial buildings once used as stores, hotels, and boarding houses. Lloyd Tolley (1902-74), for whom the road is named, kept the Chiles and Barger General Store on the ground floor of the Alhambra Hotel, the three-story cement block building that dates from 1910. The track itself may seem a bit high along here; its bed was raised several feet as part of a maintenance program in some years ago.

The gray wooden building beside the hotel was once a livery stable; it now serves as a self-storage facility. The station stood directly across the street.

At the bottom of the hill, follow Lloyd Tolley Road as it turns right to pass through a stone culvert under the tracks. Bear left as you emerge from the culvert, then turn left at the next junction (about 150 yards, just past the two-story frame house).

If you slow down or stop just beyond the house on the corner and look to the left, you'll glimpse a couple of frame houses on the hillside across the tracks. The road which once ran in front of them is gone, and the occupants now enter from the rear (Wert Faulkner Highway runs behind them). The one on the right was the railroad agent's house when the station was in use. Folks here say it was built on that spot because the caboose was located just about there when the train pulled into the station.

Drive up the hill to reach the highway; turn right and continue on through the village. The **Rockbridge County Industrial Park** is at the junction with Arnold's Valley Road (759).

The 92-acre industrial park is owned by the Rockbridge County Industrial Development Authority and is part of an organized effort to bring clean industries to the area. Ground was broken for the first company in 1989.

[Note: Arnold's Valley Road is the start of Tour 12, a closed loop through Arnold's Valley.]

Adjacent to the industrial park is the entrance to Virginia Manor, a Registered Virginia Landmark. The estate cannot be seen from the road; a good view can be had from James River Road, across the river (page 79).

East of Virginia Manor the road passes the entrance to **General Shale,** a brick manufacturing plant that closed in 1994.

> This plant was operated by its parent company in Tennessee. Its bricks were shipped all over the east coast.

Beyond General Shale, a scattering of houses announces the outskirts of the town of **Glasgow.**

> Glasgow is laid out in precise blocks, a legacy of post-Civil War development boom. General Fitzhugh Lee was president of a development company that expected to take advantage of the town's potential as a transportation center; they started their efforts later than the then-prospering Buena Vista Company, but in the end the 1893 economic depression did both companies in.
>
> The Lees Carpet Company, a division of Burlington Industries, revived the local economy with their arrival in 1935. Except for a brief period in the early 1940s, when the looms turned out cotton duck for the armed forces, folks here have been weaving carpets.

Rising behind the town is **Salling's Mountain** (1,805 feet). Its conical shape makes it easily recognizable from a distance.

> John Peter Salling, for whom the mountain is named, was a German colonist who obtained a grant of 400 acres near the confluence of the James and Maury rivers from the British Crown around 1740.

Salling's eventful life is extensively recorded in local literature, but the accounts differ wildly. He apparently set out for the Ohio River with one or two companions and was captured by Indians. He roamed the Mississippi River valley with the tribe and finally escaped, only to be captured (or purchased as an interpreter?) by the Spaniards (or was it the French?), who thought him a British spy. The ship that was to carry him to Spain (France?) for trial was intercepted by the British, who put him ashore in Charleston, South Carolina (or did he make his way to Canada, where the French governor intervened and sent him to New York?). There seems to be agreement that he walked back to his home here.

On the right, just past the grocery store, note the sign for the public boat landing on the James.

Take this rough road a quarter mile to see the picturesque confluence of the Maury and the James rivers.

In Glasgow, at Eighth and Fitz Lee Streets, is **Salling's House,** a large brick home built by Peter Salling, John's son, about 1815. It was by far the grandest house in town, and can be seen from the highway. If you want a closer look, turn left at Eight Street.

As you near the house, turn right onto Gordon Street for a look at the tiny **Salling Family Cemetery** (on a knoll to your left, about fifty yards from the corner.)

Ornate Victorian headstones mark the graves of Peter and Rebecca Salling and their son, Peter A. Salling.

A drive through the town nets a number of "boom" buildings, two hundred-year-old churches (Episcopal, 1888; Presbyterian, 1890), and contemporary dwellings. Look for the tiny town hall.

The building with the fading "Blue Ridge Tea Room" sign

also saw duty as a school and was used to train employees to run the looms while the Lees factory was under construction.

This journey ends here in Glasgow. You may wish to cross the Maury to Glasgow Highway (US 501) and go north (left) a half-mile or so to Balcony Downs, site of the Indian battle of 1742, the first such fracas in the county (see page 59). Or you may choose to go south, following the itinerary in Tour 9 to see Balcony Falls.

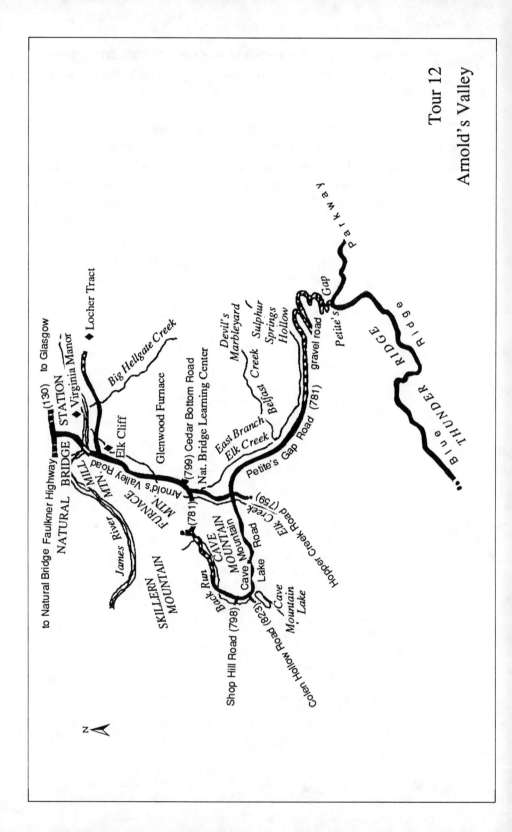

Tour 12
Arnold's Valley

Tour 12   Arnold's Valley

*A Circle Tour Beginning and Ending
in Natural Bridge Station: 10 miles*

This tour explores the remote southeastern corner of Rockbridge County—Arnold's Valley. The Blue Ridge Mountains define three sides of the valley; the fourth is bounded by the James River. Valley Road bridges the James; the only other access is a treacherous US Forest Service road that climbs Thunder Ridge to the Blue Ridge Parkway.

Most of the land you see in the valley is a part of the Jefferson National Forest. Two recreational areas are located here: the US Forest Service's Cave Mountain Lake and the privately owned James River Recreation Area campground. Picnic supplies can be bought at several country stores in the area.

There are a number of hiking and horse trails in Arnold's Valley, including a section of the Appalachian Trail high on Thunder Ridge. For maps, literature, and advice, visit the Glenwood District office of the US Forest Service on Wert Faulkner Highway (US 130), about two and a half miles east of Natural Bridge, or their seasonal information center (open from May through November) in the Natural Bridge Village complex.

BEGIN THIS JOURNEY at the junction of Wert Faulkner Highway and Valley Road (759), about three miles east of Natural Bridge Village. Valley Road curves between two hills and quickly brings you to the broad James River. Stop near the bridge to orient yourself.

The CSX Railroad tracks run under the highway bridge; the Norfolk Southern tracks cross the river on a trestle about a half-mile upstream.

Seen from the bridge, the mountains that define Arnold's Valley are very imposing. The highest, **Thunder Ridge** (3,683 feet), sweeps upward to its majestic height with no foothills to blunt its impact. A geodesic dome of the US Air Force's radar system perches on top.

Between Thunder Ridge and **Gunter Ridge** (2,691 feet) to the east is an eight-acre bald patch at about 2,000 feet. Known as the **Devil's Marbleyard,** the area is covered with round rocks of various sizes—fractured quartzite boulders. (Don't confuse it with a much larger area, nearer to you, where rock has been quarried.)

Just across the bridge, on the right side of the road, is a brick house built near the presumed site of the Greenlee Ferry. James Greenlee obtained a grant of about 550 acres here and established a ferry around 1737. In 1746 he sold some land to Charles Sinckler, and for a time the area was called Sinckler's Valley. Sinckler explored farther to the west with John Peter Salling, for whom the nearby mountain is named.

Early records show that Stephen Arnold held two tracts of land here in 1755, and the valley eventually took his name.

Once across the river, Valley Road hugs the base of **Furnace Mountain** (1,591 feet) to the west; the terrain to the east and south is rolling bottomland.

Cross the river and turn left for an interesting side trip on James River Road (782), which follows the river for a mile and a half.

The large brick house on the right, **Elk Cliff,** was the family home of US senator Miles Poindexter. His family moved back to Rockbridge when he was two years old and he lived here while attending the Fancy Hill Academy and Washington & Lee University. He moved to the state of Washington after getting his law degee from W&L, represented his adopted state in the United States senate for twelve years, was the United States ambassador to Peru 1923-28, and returned to the family homestead in 1929, living there until his death in 1946.

Poindexter collected Indian relics from the estate and nearby lands. He found a number of unfinished spearpoints and arrowheads and, given the outcroppings of flint in the area, concluded that the Indians came to this place to replenish their stock of tools and weapons.

James River Road crosses **Elk Creek** beyond Elk Cliff, then climbs high above the river. The road dips again to cross **Big Hellgate Creek** as it reaches the **James River Recreation Area,** a privately owned family campground with swimming, fishing, and other activities for RV and tent campers.

If you stop between the bridge and the camp entrance and look to your left you can glimpse **Virginia Manor,** a large white frame house across the James. (When the trees are not in full leaf, the house can be seen from the road at several points between Elk Creek and here.)

This stately private residence is a Registered Virginia Landmark. The original house (which is just a small part of the present sprawling structure) was built in 1790 by John Fleming. In the late 1800s it was home to Civil War general Fitzhugh Lee, a nephew of Robert E. Lee.

Fitzhugh Lee was governor of Virginia (1886-90) and the United States ambassador to Cuba in 1898 at the outbreak of the Spanish-American War.

George W. Stevens, president of the Chesapeake and Ohio Railroad, bought the house in the early 1900s and enlarged it considerably. He added several outbuildings, including a two-story playhouse for his children and one of the first automobile garages in the county.

Past the campground, keep bearing left as the road changes from a paved surface to gravel, and bear left again onto FS 3093. This US Forest Service road ends in a parking area at the **Locher Tract** in the Jefferson National Forest, a pleasant place to stretch your legs.

The abandoned General Shale brick manufacturing plant and Salling's Mountain are across the river from the bluff where the Locher house was located; only its chimney stands today. Fifteen or twenty minutes of easy strolling on the well-kept paths offers an enjoyable variety of ecosystems—river, wetlands, woods, and fields. The Balcony Falls Trails into the James River Face Wilderness Area starts here.

From Locher Tract, retrace your route to Valley Road and turn left. About a mile and a half beyond the river are the ruins of the **Glenwood Furnace.**

These remnants of a once-flourishing industry are the best-preserved in the county and stand right beside the road. A US Forest Service sign here states:

> Built and operated by Francis T. Anderson 1853-1865. Iron ore, charcoal and limestone were heated together, and melted iron was run into moulds of moist sand. The bars of pig iron were transported to Richmond by barges on the James River and there refined and made into cannons for the Confederacy.

Judge Anderson was the grandfather of Senator Miles Poindexter mentioned above; he owned the furnace with another laywer, David Shanks. The Tredegar Iron Works in

Richmond, where most of the Glenwood iron was consigned, was operated by the judge's brother.

A half mile south of the furnace, the road crosses the East Branch of Elk Creek and meets Back Run (781) beside the **Faith Baptist Church.** Turn right onto Back Run, which encircles **Cave Mountain** (1,652 feet), now looming ahead of you, and will bring you back to Valley Road in about four and a half miles.

This road is narrow and a bit rough, but should give you no problems in dry weather. The surface improves after the first couple of miles.

Back Run curves as it crosses Elk Creek, then climbs between Cave Mountain and **Furnace Mountain** (1,591 feet); about a half mile farther it curves sharply to the left and begins to follow **Back Run** between Cave Mountain and **Skillern Mountain** (1,719). There are a couple of side roads in the hamlet of Cave Mountain; bear left to follow Back Run as it continues to climb sharply.

As you enjoy the leisurely drive through this sparsely settled area, consider some of the people who were here long ago. In the late 1700s, Light-Horse Harry Lee, the father of General Robert E. Lee, owned property here; his land changed hands several times and is now a part of the Jefferson National Forest.

The pioneer women of Arnold's Valley are ably represented in legend of Phoebe Paxton. This steadfast wife heard of the hardships being suffered by the Revolutionary forces,so she loaded two horses with provisions and clothing produced on her farm and, with a servant, took them to her husband at Valley Forge.

Consider, too, the austerity of life in this remote valley. Edmund P. Tompkins (1868-1952), a Rockbridge doctor and historian, was appointed in 1888 to teach the Upper

Arnold's Valley school. Before the term began, he visited the place on horseback. In *Rockbridge County, Virginia, An Informal History*, he described what he found:

> It was a small log building situated on a bare bleak hillside, with no possible space for a playground. ....I found a very bare room, with no actual windows, but on each side an opening between the logs, 10" in height, 48" in length; ...The teacher was expected, at his own expense, to set 6 panes of glass, 8"x10", to let in light, and keep out cold. The ceiling, made of long split clapboards, laid shingle fashion, was just a little over 6' from the floor. I could barely stand upright. The floor was of oak boards, unplaned, about 12" broad, with plenty of crack between. The equipment consisted of a large and very rusty cast-iron stove, a very dull axe, a worn out broom, a rusty tin bucket and dipper. There were a few rickety homemade benches, no blackboards, nor anything else.

Tompkins then reports his hasty resignation of the post.

Just above the hamlet of Cave Mountain is the dam and spillway, and beyond it is the **Cave Mountain Lake Recreation Area.**

This lovely US Forest Service facility offers, for a modest fee, RV and tent camping, picnicking, hiking, and swimming from May until October.

Dr. Tompkins mentions an incident that took place here one Christmas before the lake was formed, when he was the county coroner. There was a party in a cabin located at what is now the bottom of the lake; a fight broke out, and a man was shot to death. What grist for the campfire ghost-story mill!

The road here reaches about 1,200 feet, changes its name to Cave Mountain Lake Road, and begins a two-mile descent to the valley floor (which is about 850 feet above sea level). There is logging activity in this area; watch out for trucks.

About halfway down, look for a two-story white house on the downhill side of the road. It was once an inn and is now a private residence.

Cave Mountain Lake Road again meets Arnold's Valley Road at the **Glenwood Pentecostal Holiness Church**. To the right it is called Hopper Creek Road and comes to a dead-end.

If you go straight, crossing Valley Road and continuing on Petites Gap Road (781), you can reach the Blue Ridge Parkway.

> The state-maintained road ends in two miles; a one-lane, twisting, graded, and graveled US Forest Service road climbs Thunder Ridge to the Parkway at Petite's Gap—about 2,400 feet. It should be driven with great care. In deciding whether to make this ascent, consider the weather; frequently the higher elevations will experience dense fog and clouds while the visibility in the valley is much better. The head of the trail to the Devil's Marbleyard is about a mile up this road; it is a strenuous climb.

If you turn left on Valley Road, you will be heading back out of the valley, past the **Natural Bridge Learning Center.**

> The center occupies land and buildings organized as WWI veterans' camp; for a time veterans worked at building the roads and trails in the national forest. The camp was used for a while by the Civilian Conservation Corps, and is now operated by the Virginia Department of Correctional Education as a juvenile correction facility.

Continue on Valley Road to complete your tour of the valley and get back to Wert Faulkner Highway.

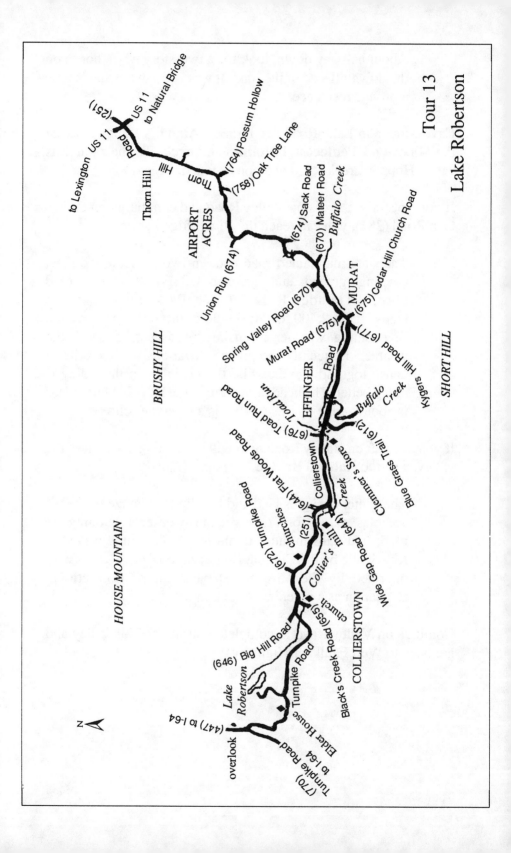

Tour 13
Lake Robertson

Lexington to Lake Robertson: 11.5 miles

Well-built and well-maintained, VA 251, called Thorn Hill Road in Lexington and Collierstown Road in the county, is a major access road to the county's western reaches, passing through Effinger and Collierstown. The road gets curvier, narrower, and hillier as you get farther out, but never alarmingly so. On sunny days it may be a little crowded, by Rockbridge standards, as folks head for Lake Robertson. The park is open from April 1 through October 31 and on fine winter Sundays. Take along a picnic—or at least some bread for the lake's resident ducks; they'll expect it!

FROM LEXINGTON take Main Street south to the traffic light at the edge of town (the Thrifty Inn is on the corner). You'll see a sign directing you to Lake Robertson; turn right (west). You're on Link Road briefly and then Thorn Hill Road. Half a mile of suburbs—and suddenly you're in the country.

In another half-mile, you may catch a glimpse of **Thorn Hill** on the hilltop to your right. (Trees obscure it in summer.) This red brick Greek Revival Style mansion was built around 1792. The historical marker here reads:

> Home of Colonel John Bowyer, an officer in the Revolutionary War, and of General E.F. Paxton, commander of the Stonewall Brigade, killed at Chancellorsville, May 3, 1863.

[Note, on the left, just past Thorn Hill, the junction with Possum Hollow (764), the beginning of Tour 14.]

A deep curve to the right and there, off to the left, looms a long, prominent ridge—**Short Hill,** at its highest about 2,630 feet.

> Shown on some maps as Short Hills, to the local people it's just Short Hill. They'll tell you, with a smile, that it is so named because the Shorts lived on one side of it and the Hills on the other. Old maps show this is so, but still ...

Then a stretch up a hill to **Airport Acres**—the valley on the right—one of the prettiest views in the county.

> The presence of a thoughtfully landscaped manufacturing plant doesn't spoil this peaceful little valley. There was a small, privately owned airport here, where the plant is, until the 1960s; it fell victim to its short runway, capricious air currents, and competition with the Roanoke airport.

A mile or so of winding road brings into view the silos of a diary farm and a broad, tranquil stretch of **Buffalo Creek.**

> Look for a great blue heron in the shallow water and a belted kingfisher on the power lines. A major watercourse, Buffalo Creek drains much of the southwestern county. Buffalo herds roamed this valley until the 18th century; now only their namesake creek wanders their former range.

Just ahead is the Dixon Bridge over Buffalo Creek, and just beyond that is **Murat.** Collierstown Road makes a sharp turn to the right here. A sign at the corner points to Lake Robertson.

> Murat (pronounced something like *mew-rah*) consists entirely of the sign bearing its name. There was once a post office here (1884-1940). Local legend says that W.H. Bowlin, the postmaster, named the substation for his cat,

who was called Murat after Napoleon's flamboyant general.

Rocky, burbling Buffalo Creek is now on your right. In about a mile, the road again crosses the Buffalo where it comes down from the western highlands to gather up **Collier's Creek.**

Another half-mile along Collier's Creek brings you to the junction with the Bluegrass Trail (612) (Tour 15) on the left and the community of **Effinger.**

> Effinger includes an elementary school and a volunteer fire department with a large, modern firehouse. The sizable white building across the Collier's Creek bridge was once a high school; now it's a private residence. Effinger serves as a social center for this area. Folks come from miles around to suppers and dances, cakewalks and carnivals at the school and firehouse.
>
> Effinger School's name honors George W. Effinger, who, from 1876 to 1926, served as a teacher, then as school superintendent, and finally as chairman of the Rockbridge County Board of Education.

Across the bridge, turn left to continue on Collierstown Road. A few hundred yards brings you to **Clemmer's Store,** on the left, where you can buy food and gas and, in the tradition of country stores, just about anything else you need.

> This building began life (date unknown) as Painter's Mill. If you stop at the store, stroll over for a look at Collier's Creek and you'll see the narrow stream channel and steep walls that made it such a good location for a waterwheel.
>
> Past Effinger, notice the various means that residents have contrived to cross Collier's Creek to their homes on the other side.

Stay on Collierstown Road as it makes a sharp turn to the right where Wide Gap Road (644) continues straight, going over an old truss bridge. Beside it is the **Wade-McCaleb Mill,** built in the 1920s and now a private residence.

> The first mill on this site was built in 1779 by John Collier. The creek and town were probably named for the Collier family, although it is true that colliers (charcoal-makers) at the Lucy Selina iron furnace across North Mountain made their homes here.

In another mile and a half you'll pass the first of Collierstown's three churches—**Collierstown Baptist Church,** built in 1960 after the merger of two small congregations. Just down the road (and almost *in* the road) is the **Collierstown United Methodist Church,** built about 1840.

Bear left just beyond the churches. Now you are on Turnpike Road (672). [Tour 16 begins here.]

Ahead on the left is **Hostetter's Store,** your last chance to get picnic supplies (machine-dispensed snacks and soft drinks may be the only food available at Lake Robertson).

Then, on the left, **Collierstown Presbyterian Church.**

> A stop here will reward you handsomely. Built in 1856, this sturdy Greek Revival Style church has an especially interesting Greek-key design carved into the wooden lintels over the windows. Drive up the lane that skirts the hillside cemetery behind the church. The sweeping vista—Brushy Mountain, Short Hill, and House Mountain, the soaring Alleghenies and, below you, the Collier's Creek valley—provides an impressive overview of regional geography, as well as a stunningly beautiful scene.
>
> The cemetery has been in use since 1856. Tombstones bear

the names of families that were among the area's early settlers—Goodbar, Potter, Cummings, Clark, Nicely, Hotinger, Hostetter, Reid, and many more—and whose descendants still live here.

Continue on Turnpike Road about two-tenths of a mile, and then follow it as it turns left onto the concrete bridge over Collier's Creek, where a sign points the way to **Lake Robertson**. A country mile brings you to the park entrance.

This 581-acre mountainside park provides excellent recreational facilities: a fifty-three-site campground; picnic areas; twelve miles of woodland hiking trails; a thirty-one-acre boating and fishing lake; playgrounds, tennis court, swimming pool, even a softball field. The lake was created by damming a system of springs and streams, part of the headwaters of Collier's Creek. Its steep, rocky contours and icy springs preclude swimming. At its deepest end, about thirty-five feet down, lie the buildings of a drowned farm.

Opened in 1973, the park is owned by the State Game Commission and operated by Rockbridge County. The park's name honors Lexington's A. Willis Robertson (1887-1971), for many terms a US congressman and then senator and an ardent outdoorsman and conservationist (and father of evangelist Pat Robertson).

The tour ends here. Return to Lexington by the route that brought you, or check the master map for other options.

A LITTLE ADDED ADVENTURE: For a challenging extension to this tour, turn right as you leave the park for a scenic four-mile journey up **North Mountain** (3,400 feet). Please read all of the following description before you decide to try it. The road is not dauntingly steep, but it is gravel and narrow, and you will be climbing about 1,500 feet. Don't make this drive in wet weather.

This route was part of the Lexington-Covington Turnpike (see Tour 16). Farmers hauling produce to Covington and Clifton Forge took along an extra team of horses. The steeds that pulled the wagon to the mountaintop were turned loose to find their way home, while the second team continued the journey.

About a mile from the park, pause at a driveway entrance on the right for a look at **Elder House.** (Please don't go up the driveway; this is a private residence.)

> The house, dating from the late 18th century, was built of rough fieldstone and river jacks (smooth stones from a river bed). Even from a distance the alternating courses, light and dark, give this house an unusual character.

The turnpike now becomes a gravel road and climbs steadily. A scant half-mile brings you to the junction with Hayslette Road (654), an easy drive that will return you to Turnpike Road near Collierstown. Or, bear right to continue up the mountain. The road becomes quite narrow. If you meet another vehicle, one of you may have to back up.

In just under two and a half miles you'll encounter a hairpin turn to the left. Stop at the small parking area here.

> This vantage point (2,777 feet) offers sweeping views of the county, even when the trees are in leaf. And speaking of leaves, be careful of the abundant poison ivy.

The road now becomes very steep, rocky, and rutted. In about half a mile an unmarked dirt road goes to the right; keep on the left. Just ahead is the junction with FS 447, a good gravel road. (Turnpike Road turns sharply to the left here.) Turn right onto 447 and continue eight-tenths of a mile to an overlook on the right.

You have earned a spectacular reward! From this elevation (3,000 feet) it seems as if all the county is in view.

You can return the way you came; or continue on 447 about six miles to its junction with the Midland Trail (850) and I-64's exit 11 (15 miles from Lexington); or backtrack to the junction and follow Turnpike Road about four miles to I-64's exit 10 (23 miles from Lexington).

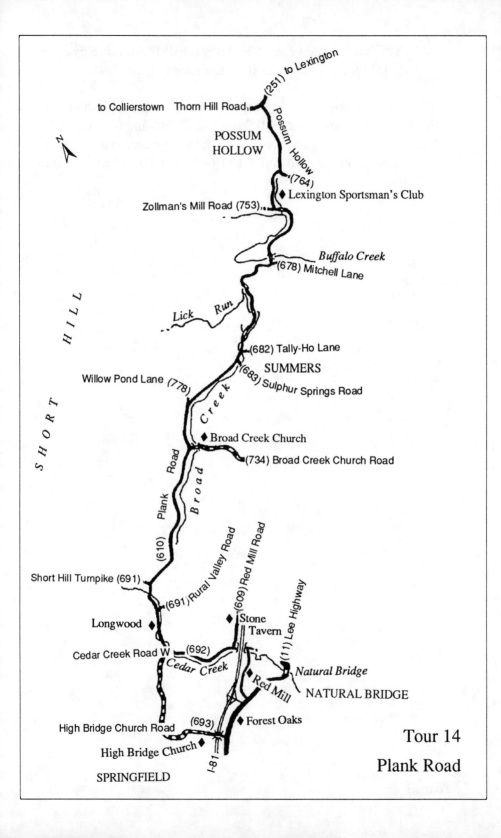

(251) to Lexington

to Collierstown   Thorn Hill Road

POSSUM
HOLLOW

Possum Hollow

(764)

♦ Lexington Sportsman's Club

Zollman's Mill Road (753)

Buffalo Creek

(678) Mitchell Lane

Lick Run

(682) Tally-Ho Lane

SUMMERS

(683) Sulphur Springs Road

Willow Pond Lane (778)

Creek

♦ Broad Creek Church

(734) Broad Creek Church Road

Broad

Road

Plank

(610)

(691) Rural Valley Road

(609) Red Mill Road

(11) Lee Highway

Short Hill Turnpike (691)

Longwood ♦

♦ Stone
Tavern

Natural Bridge

Cedar Creek Road W   (692)

NATURAL BRIDGE

Cedar Creek

Red Mill

High Bridge Church Road   (693)

♦ Forest Oaks

High Bridge Church ♦

I-81

SPRINGFIELD

SHORT HILL

N

Tour 14

Plank Road

Tour 14   Plank Road

Possum Hollow to High Bridge: 18.5 miles

This excursion will take you through rural Broad Creek valley along the eastern base of Short Hill. The road twists and turns as it follows meandering creeks, but there are few hills and the trip is one even the driver can enjoy.

FROM LEXINGTON, take Main Street south to the traffic light at the edge of town (the Thrifty Inn is on the corner). Turn right (west) on Link Road, which becomes Thorn Hill Road for about a mile and a half to Possum Hollow (764), on the left. This trip follows the Bicentennial Bicycle Route; its black-and-white signs with the bicycle symbol will help keep you on course.

Possum Hollow pulls away from the junction in a series of curves that follow **Possum Run** as it courses through **Possum Hollow.** The road is narrow, and with several homes very near the road, the twenty-mph limit on the curves is a realistic one.

In about a mile, the road forks; bear right onto Plank Road (610), following the bicycle route sign.

> The large yellow building to your left is the **Lexington Sportsmans Club,** an excellent place to do some birdwatching along the banks of Possum Run.
>
> In the mid-1800s, wooden planks were laid on wooden

stringers along this low-lying road to provide a smooth, mud-free surface for traffic, a practice then popular on the east coast. The planking was not, however, a cure-all. In 1864, as Union troops departed Lexington along this route, one soldier noted that the road was "rough, crooked, and rocky, with occasional deep holes."

Plank Road crosses Possum Run just before the little watercourse empties into **Buffalo Creek,** follows the creek beside a brush-covered limestone cliff, crosses the Buffalo on a wide bridge, and heads upstream along a third watercourse, **Broad Creek.**

This creek runs parallel to **Short Hill,** a rugged ridge that reaches a height of 2,630 feet and forms a majestic backdrop for the farms scattered throughout the Broad Creek valley.

About a half mile south of the bridge is a double S-curve posted at 25 mph; the road is narrow, and visibility is severely restricted. Be alert for slow-moving farm machinery.

About a mile south of the curve you will come upon one of the beautifully constructed stone souvenirs left to the county by the **Valley Railroad.**

An expensive, ill-fated project that was never completed, the Valley Railroad was to have been the first railway in Rockbridge County and would have connect Lexington with Staunton to the north and Salem to the south. It was planned during the Reconstruction boom and begun just before the financial crash of 1893. In the end, it cost the county a couple of million dollars, and the portion actually completed was dismantled for scrap. The bonds that financed the fiasco were finally paid off and burned in a public ceremony in 1922.

Heavy masonry culverts, fills, and abutments are scattered along the old railroad grade from one end of the county to the other. The remnants you see along this road are the most accessible.

About a mile past the bridge, at Sulphur Springs Road (683), on the right, is what's left of a mill that was once part of **Summers.**

> This little community boasted a post office, store, mill, school, and smithy. Only the remnants of the mill now mark its place.

A mile and a half farther south, look for a board fence on the right; behind it is a stand of loblolly pines. Just ahead is the junction with Broad Creek Church Road (734). Turn left to visit the **Broad Creek ARP Church.**

> Built around 1849, this small brick building nestles in a little wooded vale. Its well-kept cemetery, about a half mile beyond the church, dates from 1840.

As you continue southward and the road climbs gently uphill, you will notice Broad Creek narrowing, until it disappears altogether. At Rural Valley Road (691), you will have reached the upper end of Broad Creek valley. Here begins the gentle descent along **Cedar Creek.**

> Plank Road crosses Cedar Creek several times. The creek rises high on Short Hill and flows beneath the Natural Bridge on its way to the James River.

About a half mile past Rural Valley Road, on the right, is a large brick house.

> A sign at the gate identifies **Longwood** (1868), a bed-and-breakfast inn. With its two-story, pillared portico, the house is reminiscent of Scarlett O'Hara's *Tara.*

Just south of Longwood, turn left onto Cedar Creek Road West

(692) to follow Cedar Creek. (The bicycle route also turns here.) In about a mile, turn left onto Red Mill Road (609), (just before the I-81 overpass). In about a half mile, on the left, is the **Stone Tavern.**

> The Valley Road, once the main highway, passed along here. Many visitors to the Natural Bridge stayed in this comfortable tavern, which was built in the late 1700s. Thomas Jefferson, who owned the bridge, was one of many guests who signed his name on the building. Jefferson scratched his name on window glass (since broken). Daniel Boone wrote his name in the plaster and dated it May 19, 1816.

Return to Cedar Creek West, turn left to pass under I-81, and follow Red Mill Road as it curves sharply to the right. Just around the bend, on the creek, is the **Red Mill.**

> Once the hub of the Cedar Creek settlement, the mill was built in 1765 by William Poague and was purchased by Hugh Barclay in 1770. Barclay painted the mill red and built an inn beside it. Today the brick-and-stone inn is a private residence.

> Although Lee Highway now carries the county's north-south traffic over Cedar Creek on the Natural Bridge, early travelers used the Valley Road, which forded the creek here, at the Red Mill. (See Trip 10 for more information about the Valley Road.)

From the Red Mill, the road climbs gently upward to a stop sign at Lee Highway (US 11). Turn right (south) and follow the highway's service road (F 055), which parallels the interstate. About a half mile south, look for **Forest Oaks** on the left.

> This house was at the north end of an unrealized dream. The town of **Springfield** was to have been laid out from John McConkey's land to the Great Road (another name for the

Valley Road) leading from Lexington to Buchanan (then Pattonsburg). The court recorded McConkey's plan in 1797, and some houses were built, but the town never reached its potential.

Although Springfield didn't endure, many pioneers passed through here on their way west. Daniel Boone supposedly had a rifle made for him at Siler's gunshop, then brought it back to be fitted with a new stock when the original burned in a cabin fire. George Washington is reported to have visited a compatriot (local resident Captain Audley Paul) who fought with him at Braddock's Defeat. Audley, the brother of naval hero John Paul Jones, supposedly left home under a cloud and dropped the Jones to lower his profile in the new world.

Daniel Hech built wagons here for fifty years (1812-1862); some of his wagons crossed the continent to California. Hech's brother and some friends emigrated to Springfield, Ohio, which they named after their Virginia home.

A cherry tree once held a sign proclaiming Springfield as the center of Virginia. It is 200 miles to Abingdon, Harpers Ferry, Wheeling, and Albemarle. What little there was left of Springfield was pretty much destroyed when I-81 was built in the mid-1960s.

Drive a few hundred yards farther south to High Bridge Church Road (693), and cross the interstate. **High Bridge Presbyterian Church** stands atop a hill just across the bridge.

The congregation was organized in 1770. This stately church with its red brick and white trim was built in 1903 and enlarged in 1922.

The Reverend Samuel Houston pastored this flock from 1796 to 1839. He fought unscathed in the Revolutionary

War and was cousin to the Sam Houston (born in Rockbridge) who made his name in Texas (see pages 3-4).

This tour ends at High Bridge Church. You can return to Lexington via Lee Highway or I-81.

If you'd like to retrace Plank Road back to Lexington, continue on High Bridge Church Road along Spring Gap Creek; bear right at the bottom of the hill (where the road crosses the creek). You will be on Plank Road—the part that you missed when you turned to go to the Red Mill.

Effinger to Rapps Mill—A Circle Tour: 18 miles

This excursion explores the sparsely settled southwestern corner of the county, following South Buffalo Creek along the slopes of Short Hill and crossing to North Buffalo for the return trip. The driving is easy, the scenery lovely.

FROM LEXINGTON, take Thorn Hill Road (VA 251), following the directions in Tour 13 to Effinger, and turn left onto Bluegrass Trail (612), a well-marked junction just before the school and firehouse.

> Almost immediately, on the left, Buffalo Creek roils in a deep horseshoe bend around the north end of Short Hill as it makes its way across the county to join the Maury River.

The road follows the creek upstream for about a mile, where you'll see, on the right, the junction with Oxford Lane (677). Turn right for a visit to **Oxford Presbyterian Church.** The lane ends in about a third of a mile at the church and surrounding farms.

> If this seems like a lonely location, remember that many rural churches were built wherever local landowners donated the land for them.

> Oxford Church was established about 1768 (its earliest records are lost). The present building, the third on this site, was constructed in 1868-69, largely by soldiers back from

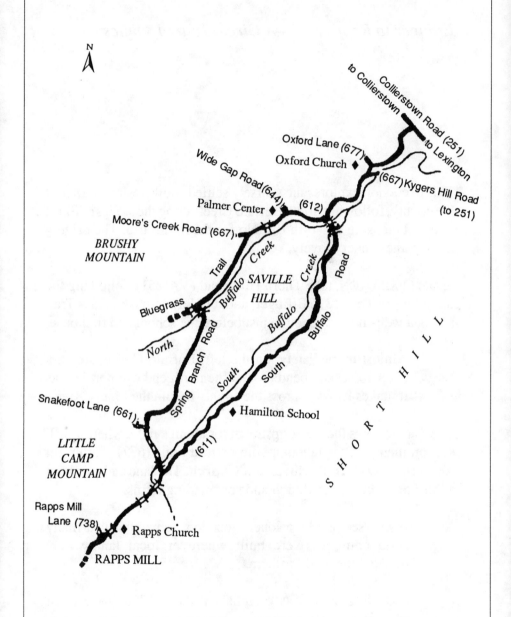

N

Collierstown Road (251)
to Collierstown
to Lexington
(667) Kygers Hill Road
(to 251)

Oxford Lane (677)
Oxford Church ◆

Wide Gap Road (644)

Palmer Center ◆   (612)

Moore's Creek Road (667)

*BRUSHY
MOUNTAIN*

Trail

Creek

Buffalo

*SAVILLE
HILL*

Creek

Road

Bluegrass

North

Spring Branch Road

South

South

Buffalo

South

Buffalo

S   H   O   R   T   H   I   L   L

Snakefoot Lane (661)

*LITTLE
CAMP
MOUNTAIN*

◆ Hamilton School

(611)

Rapps Mill
Lane (738)

◆ Rapps Church

RAPPS MILL

Tour 15
Two Buffalos

the Civil War. The impressive view from the church takes in the top half of Short Hill to the south and the tops of Big House and Little House mountains to the north.

The Oxford cemetery includes graves as old as 1858. One monument remembers the mother and five children of a pioneer family that lived in the saddle between Big House and Little House; they perished during a blizzard in 1846.

Return to Bluegrass Trail and turn right. Bear right as you pass the junction with Kygers Hill Road. In about two miles you may be able to see, on the left, the place where North and South Buffalo creeks join to form Buffalo Creek.

Just beyond is the junction with South Buffalo Road (611) at a bridge over North Buffalo Creek. Turn left onto this bridge.

South Buffalo Road ascends the South Buffalo valley, crossing and recrossing the stream as it winds between Short Hill and the adjacent highlands. The road climbs very gently from an elevation of about 1, 150 feet at the bridge to 1, 450 feet at Rapps Church.

Three and a half miles up this valley is a one-room log schoolhouse. Watch carefully for **Hamilton School,** on the left, just around the bend.

Constructed in 1823 by a devout citizen as both "a house of publick worship" and a school, this structure served the surrounding neighborhood for more than a hundred years. It is privately owned and not open to the public, but you can get a close look from the gate. The plank door was used as a community bulletin board. In the schoolyard, a teacher—a wounded Confederate veteran—once drilled the older boys who would themselves soon become Confederate recruits.

Closed in 1928 because of the dwindling number of

students, the building fell into decay. In the 1950s it was restored to its present fine condition.

Two miles beyond the schoool, note on the right the junction with Spring Branch Road at a bridge over South Buffalo Creek. But continue on South Buffalo Road another mile to **Rapps Church.**

> The village that once thrived around Rapps Mill became a Methodist preaching center in 1836. Rapps Church was built in 1900 as a nondenominational community church. It is now administered as an outpost of Oxford Presbyterian Church, but with its own loyal and diligent congregation. The cemetery includes the graves of Mathias Rapp (1808-1880) and his wife, Mary Saville Rapp (1814-1888), who donated the land for the cemetery and church.
>
> Mathias Rapp was another Rockbridge inventor. He devised and patented a turbine-driven milling mechanism.

Just over the hill, in the little community of **Rapps Mill,** is **Marshall's** grocery and gas station. If you continue south from here, you'll reach the Botetourt County line in about three miles, and US 11 in another seven miles.

To continue this tour, backtrack on South Buffalo Road just over a mile to Spring Branch Road, turn left across the bridge you noted earlier, and drive along wooded hillsides to the North Buffalo Creek valley.

In less than a mile, Snakefoot Lane (661), wanders off to the left. A county map that hangs in the Rockbridge Regional Library indicates that the entire valley of the Buffalo was once called Snakefoot. Continue right on Spring Branch Road. In another mile or so you'll see on the left the clustered silos of one of the country's largest dairy farms. The hill on your right is **Saville Hill** (about 1,700 feet), named for an early family (including Mary Saville Rapp) whose descendants still live in the county.

Spring Branch Road ends at its junction with Bluegrass Trail and North Buffalo Creek. Turn right to follow the creek downstream through the North Buffalo Creek Valley.

In three miles you'll pass the **Palmer Community Center.**

> Local people still call this Palmer School. Built in 1903 by citizens of the area, the school was operated as Palmer Academy. In 1906 it became Rockbridge County's first rural high school. It was here that the former pupils of Hamilton School came after 1928, until Effinger Elementary School was established. The building now hosts meetings of the Travel Club, the Extension Homemakers Club, and other groups.

Just ahead is the junction with South Buffalo Road (and the confluence of the two Buffalos), and you've completed the loop. Follow Bluegrass Trail to the left to return to your starting point.

Two miles brings you to a fork in the road. Bear left to stay on Bluegrass Trail to return to Effinger. (If you take the right fork, Kygers Hill Road, you can reach Collierstown Road at Murat by way of Kyger Hill.)

In either case, turn right onto Collierstown Road to return to Lexington, or consult the master map for other options.

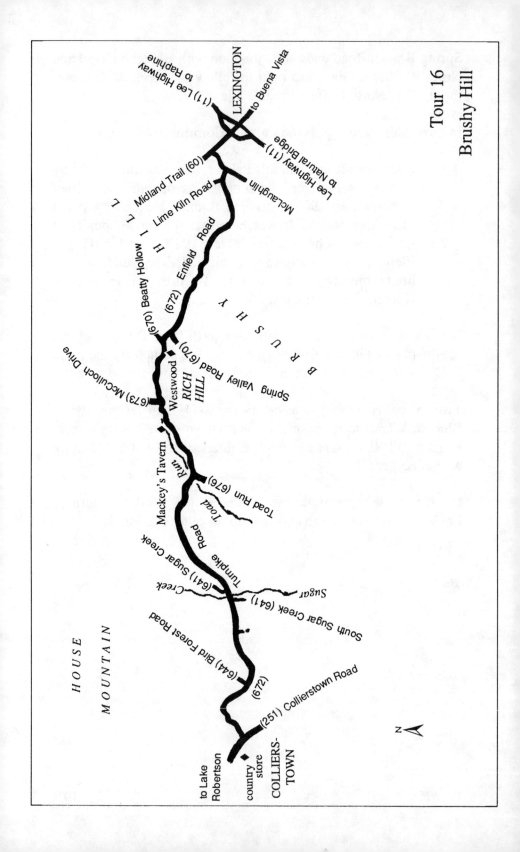

Tour 16
Brushy Hill

Lexington to Collierstown: 10 miles

Turnpike Road (672) is the extension of Enfield Road in Lexington. This hard-surfaced, two-lane country road climbs Brushy Hill, crosses Toad Run, passes through beautiful, sweeping pasturelands, and ends its journey in Collierstown. The route was part of the old Lexington-Covington Turnpike.

FROM LEXINGTON, take Nelson Street (US 60) west. Turn left on Glasgow Street at Washington and Lee's Lenfest Arts Center, just before the old railroad bridge that now serves foot traffic. Glasgow climbs a little hill past the old train station and merges with McLaughlin; continue on over the hill on McLaughlin, then turn right onto Lime Kiln Road, which crosses **Woods Creek.**

In about half a mile, at the Y-intersection, bear left onto Enfield.

> As you leave the city limits you'll see the Art Deco Style water tank and water filtration plant to the right.

About three-quarters of a mile from the city limits, look back over your shoulder for a postcard-view of Lexington nestled among the hills. From here the road makes its way along the timber-clad slopes of **Brushy Hill** as it climbs towards a saddle.

> Brushy Hill is a ridge with a series of peaks; the highest point (to your left) is 1,955 feet; to your right it reaches

1,740 feet; the road itself climbs no higher than about 1,550 feet through a saddle.

In 1864, as Union troops descended upon Lexington, one unit crossed the Maury River at Rockbridge Baths and circled to invade the town from the west. Brushy Hill was thick with marauding Union soldiers. One current Rockbridge resident has a piece of china that belonged to her great-grandmother, who saved it from the Yankees by dropping it into the pig-slop barrel in the barnyard. The barrel was a popular hiding place; knowing soldiers listened for the clink of silver as they stirred the slops. The platter made no noise and thus was spared.

General Robert E. Lee rode his horse, Traveller, all over Rockbridge County and was frequently seen on Brushy Hill. The same great-grandmother who outfoxed the Yankees reported that the general enjoyed a cold glass of buttermilk and a friendly conversation.

About two and a half miles along is a stop sign at Spring Valley Road (670 to the left) and Beatty Hollow (670 to the right); bear left to continue on Turnpike Road (672). You have crossed Brushy Hill and are headed downhill, toward **Walter's Creek.** At the bottom of the hill, look for a large house to the left.

Westwood (about 1835) was built by Robert Wilson in the Classical Revival Style. The brick house sits on a knoll some distance from the road. Its sweeping lawns are guarded by a cordon of large trees.

Past Westwood, the road emerges from the hills and traverses an area of gently rolling fields. **Rich Hill** (1,864 feet) is to the south, on your left. In about a mile and and a half is Mackey's Tavern.

A stone house and outbuildings very close to the road, Mackey's Tavern was built in the late 18th century as an inn and toll-collection point on the well-travelled Lexington-Covington Turnpike. It is now a private residence. The wooden section was added in 1883.

The little creek that crosses beneath the road just before Mackey's tavern and then flows beside it is the upper end of **Toad Run.**

This run is named for a German family named Todd who settled in this area; they pronounced their name with a long O, and Todd's Run eventually became Toad Run. Samuel Todd was a miller; his mill was north of here, on Kerr's Creek, just above Whistle Creek (page 112).

Samuel Todd's daughter, Jane Todd Crawford, and Ephraim McDowell, the grandson of Captain John McDowell, one of the original settlers in Rockbridge, together made medical history. Jane Todd married a Rockbridge man and they emigrated to the western frontier—Kentucky—and settled about sixty miles from Danville. Ephraim McDowell, meanwhile, studied medicine in Staunton, Virginia, and Edinburgh, Scotland, then headed for the frontier and set up a practice in Danville.

Jane developed an abdominal tumor and consulted her fellow Virginian, who suggested what was then an extremely dangerous treatment: surgery. She agreed, and on December 25, 1809, strapped to a table in the doctor's house and dosed with whiskey and laudanum (the strongest anesthetics known at the time), underwent a twenty-five-minute operation that delivered her of a twenty-two-pound tumor—the first ovariotomy performed in the United States. The patient was cured, and the doctor went on to be recognized as the Father of Abdominal Surgery. (See page 6—there is a memorial to Dr. McDowell near his birthplace.)

Turnpike Road meanders westward through relatively open land

and wooded hillsides favored by deer. Just below the junction with Sugar Creek Road (641), the road crosses **Sugar Creek** itself, which rises on **House Mountain** (3,645 feet, and behind you at this point).

> A gracious old farmhouse perches above the road, overlooking the creek and several outbuildings, including a photogenic red barn.

Between here and Collierstown (just under two miles), there are several interesting views of House Mountain. Woodlands alternate with grassy fields to give a rich texture to the landscape.

> The numerous deep hollows are ancient **sinkholes.** These occurred with the collapse of caves and channels created by the action of water flowing through the permeable sandstone that underlies much of this region.

> In the distance, you can see the Collierstown Presbyterian Church, its cemetery spread across the hill behind it (see pages 88-89).

The stop sign just before Hostetter's store signals your arrival at the end of this tour: **Collierstown.**

> Across from the store a set of cement steps climbs the bank, marking the spot where an inn and toll-collection point once stood. From here the Lexington-Covington Turnpike climbed North Mountain, a challenge for man and beast (see page 90).

You can turn right to Lake Robertson (about two miles farther west) and North Mountain, or turn left to return to Lexington via Collierstown Road (VA 251), about 10 miles (see Tour 13).

Tour 17   Westward Ho!

Lexington to Rockbridge Alum Springs: 15 miles

The Midland Trail (now US 60) once carried travelers from the Tidewater region of Virginia to the western frontier—West Virginia, Kentucky, and Tennessee. I-64 now does the job for those in a hurry to be someplace else. If you want to travel at a more leisurely pace, come with us. At the end of the tour is Rockbridge Alum Springs, an historic spa that now operates year-round as a camp for high school students. It's not open to the public, but if you want to visit, please call ahead for an appointment (703) 977-9276.

FROM LEXINGTON, follow Nelson Street (US 60) west—past Lenfest Arts Center, past the Washington & Lee University athletic fields and the ruins of Liberty Hall, W&L's forerunner.

For a brief but interesting side trip, turn left onto Borden Road, which will take you through a residential area to the **Lime Kiln Arts** open-air theater (an identifying sign hangs at its entrance from May to October). On a hilltop to the west is the Art Deco Style water tower.

> Around the turn of the 20th century, this hollow hummed with the production of lime from the very bedrock of the county. The throbbing vibrations of the quarrying operation and the roar of charcoal-fired limekilns once sounded here. Now, however, the vibrations are more likely to come from musicians encouraged by the roar of the crowd. Tables are

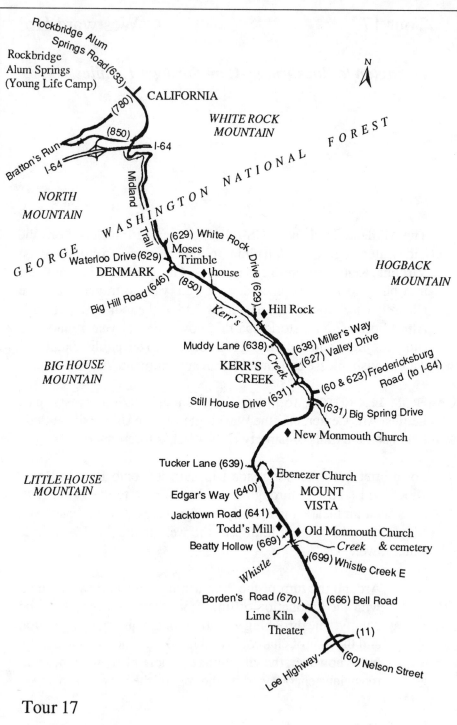

Rockbridge Alum Springs Road (633)

Rockbridge Alum Springs (Young Life Camp)

(780) CALIFORNIA

WHITE ROCK MOUNTAIN

N

(850)

I-64

Bratton's Run

I-64

Midland Trail

GEORGE WASHINGTON NATIONAL FOREST

NORTH MOUNTAIN

(629) White Rock Drive

Waterloo Drive (629)

Moses Trimble house

DENMARK

HOGBACK MOUNTAIN

Big Hill Road (646)

(850)

(629)

Hill Rock

Kerr's

Muddy Lane (638)

(638) Miller's Way

(627) Valley Drive

BIG HOUSE MOUNTAIN

KERR'S CREEK

Creek

(60 & 623) Fredericksburg Road (to I-64)

Still House Drive (631)

(631) Big Spring Drive

New Monmouth Church

Tucker Lane (639)

LITTLE HOUSE MOUNTAIN

Ebenezer Church

Edgar's Way (640)

MOUNT VISTA

Jacktown Road (641)

Todd's Mill

Beatty Hollow (669)

Old Monmouth Church

Creek & cemetery

(699) Whistle Creek E

Whistle

Borden's Road (670)

(666) Bell Road

Lime Kiln Theater

(11)

(60) Nelson Street

Lee Highway

Tour 17

Westward Ho!

available for pre-show picnics, and popcorn and drinks are sold near show time.

Turn right, away from the theater gate, and take Bell Road (666) half a mile back to the highway; turn left (west). Here, near the **Keydet General Motel,** is the first of the many excellent views of **House Mountain** that await you on this journey.

About a mile past the motel, the road dips to cross **Whistle Creek** at the intersection with Whistle Creek South (669)

Local legend tell us that Whistle Creek may at first have been called Cain't Whistle (or No Whistle) Creek, a wry commentary on the abililities of the man who first saw it.

Pull off the road just past the creek (at Whistle Creek South, on the right) to visit the **Old Monmouth Cemetery** and the ruins of **Old Monmouth Presbyterian Church.**

In 1745, a log building known as Hall's Meeting House or Forks-of-the-James was erected here, on the hillside just above the creek. It was the first Presbyterian church south of the Maury (then called North) River and served the whole area between the Maury and James rivers. (That included Lexington, which even as late as 1780 had but six houses.) A stone church built in 1788 was used until 1852; a part of one wall still stands. In 1852 the congregation removed to New Monmouth, which you will see about two and a half miles west of here.

(When Lexington Presbyterian Church was built, a stone from Old Monmouth, the mother church, was embedded in its front wall.)

Old Monmouth Cemetery was used from 1749 to 1933. The northern portion contains the graves of slaves.

There are two historical markers here, one about the church and one about Jane Todd Crawford, who was born nearby (and whose story is told on page 107).

A little farther west, across from **Kelly's Corner** country store, are the remnants of the mill run by Jane's father, Samuel Todd.

> **Todd's Mill** was frequently used as a landmark when describing the location of something in this area. Toad Run, a well-known watercourse to the south of here, is named for Samuel Todd.
>
> Mills flourished all over the county, but of special interest in this area was the establishment of a neighborhood industry to clean and card the fleece from Rockbridge sheep. The wool was spun and knitted into socks and jackets, or dyed and woven into bedspreads (or "kivvers"). A map made by VMI cadets in 1858 shows a "woollen factory" near here. Sheep are still raised in the county; their surefootedness is suited to the steep hillsides. Their fleece is no longer processed here.

A mile and a half beyond Kelly's Corner, on a hillside, the twin-towered **Ebenezer Associate Reformed Presbyterian Church** faces the road.

> Organized in 1790 as the House Mountain Meeting House, the congregation changed its name to Ebenezer in 1825, then moved to this Gothic frame building in 1899. Its cemetery is beside the road.

About a mile and a half farther along is **New Monmouth Presbyterian Church,** on the right.

> The 1842 Gothic brick building sits high on a hilltop, surrounded by wooded mountain slopes in a setting that inspires awe. The oldest tombstones in its hillside cemetery

are clustered near the church, as they are in most country church graveyards.

A scant mile along, the road turns west again and crosses **Kerr's Creek.** Signs tell you that US 60 turns to the right here to follow the interstate west. Don't turn; continue straight on Midland Trail.

Just past the intersection is the little community of **Kerr's Creek** with its fairgrounds, volunteer fire department, and a scattering of homes.

To the right is the double-humped silhouette of **Hogback Mountain.** Ahead is **House Mountain,** which was rescued from possible development in 1989 by the efforts of a coalition of local groups. (This concern was not unprecedented. Some years ago another group of citizens intervened to prevent a logging company from defacing Jump Mountain with irresponsible harvesting techniques.)

Just past the intersection of Valley Drive (627) are the ruins of **Miller's Mill,** built about 1816.

Beyond the mill, look for the junction withWhite Rock Drive (629).

On the right is **Hill Rock,** an 1850s plantation house that departed from the Classical Revival Style popular back then. The unusual bracketed roof and cut-out porch supports are visible from the road.

Less than a mile farther west, set back from the road, on the right, is the **Moses Trimble House.**

This brick house, built around 1800, stands on a low hill, with **White Rock Mountain** (3,345 feet) rising behind it. Heavy white pillars make the house easy to recognize.

Farther west, at the intersection with Big Hill Road, is the farming community of **Denmark.**

This hamlet felt the wrath of a band of Shawnee Indians in the mid-1700s. No first-hand records of the tragedies have been found, but local legend tells of two raids in this area (between Denmark and Kerr's Creek), one in 1763 and another in 1765, during which a number of settlers were killed and taken prisoner.

From Denmark, the road curves to the northwest, away from House Mountain, skirts the base of **North Mountain** (3,400 feet) to the west, and begins to climb gently.

About two miles beyond Denmark the Midland Trail climbs seriously as it switches between North and White Rock mountains. As you climb, look off to your left for some lovely and unusual views of House Mountain. If the foliage permits, you may catch a glimpse of the I-64 bridge high above and ahead of you—your destination. At 2,086 feet the road crests the pass and slips beneath the bridge.

The view from the top is breathtaking. Back to the east is House Mountain; to the west is the valley of **Bratton's Run,** which reaches northward toward Goshen.

This journey ends here on the mountains pass, the highest point of the drive. There are two ways to return to Lexington:

- retrace this route, if only to be pleasantly surprised by different aspects of the mountains;

- or hop on the interstate and zip back to Lexington. To do so, continue on the Midland Trail over the mountain about a half-mile to the well-marked I-64 interchange.

A LITTLE ADDED ADVENTURE: If the beauty of these mountains—the dramatic slopes, the pleasant mix of hardwoods and fragrant pines, and fresh mountain breezes—tempts you to remain a little longer, let us take you to Rockbridge Alum Springs, about four miles from here over some fairly rough roads.

Continue on Midland Trail past the interstate entrance and turn right in about a half-mile, onto Bratton's Run Road (780). Half a mile brings you to Alum Springs Road (633); turn left.

> The handful of houses at the intersection comprise **California,** named for an iron forge. This area is also known as Pettytown for the numerous Petty family relations hereabouts.

Rock Bridge Alum Road is not paved, but with patience you will reach, in about a mile and a half, the sign at the entrance of **Rockbridge Alum Springs,** which now operates as a camp.

> Access to the Young Life camp is limited. If you didn't make an appointment, there may not be a staff person available to show you around.

> Rockbridge Alum Springs was second in popularity only to White Sulphur Springs in this region; as many as 1,800 guests vacationed here at one time. They praised the curative powers of the alum-laced water, which was bottled and sold to those unable to make the trip.

> The whole spa scene began to fade when the automobile made it possible for people to move about easily; it was no longer so appealing to stay in just one spot for the entire vacation period. Virginia Military Institute ran a summer school here from about 1910 to 1920; the hotel was kept open, but the number of guests diminished until it was no longer profitable.

To get back to Lexington, retrace your route, following either option given above.

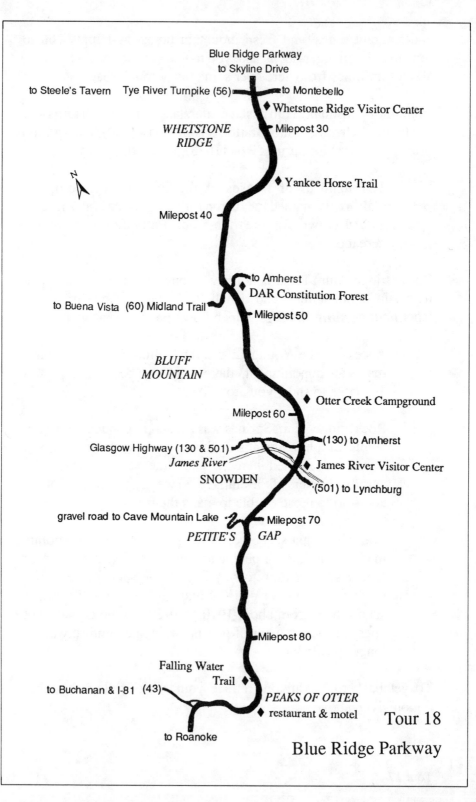

Blue Ridge Parkway
to Skyline Drive

to Steele's Tavern   Tye River Turnpike (56)   to Montebello

◆ Whetstone Ridge Visitor Center

WHETSTONE RIDGE

Milepost 30

N

◆ Yankee Horse Trail

Milepost 40

to Amherst
◆ DAR Constitution Forest
to Buena Vista (60) Midland Trail
Milepost 50

BLUFF MOUNTAIN

◆ Otter Creek Campground

Milepost 60

(130) to Amherst

Glasgow Highway (130 & 501)
James River   ◆ James River Visitor Center
SNOWDEN
(501) to Lynchburg

gravel road to Cave Mountain Lake   Milepost 70
PETITE'S   GAP

Milepost 80

Falling Water
Trail ◆
to Buchanan & I-81 (43)   *PEAKS OF OTTER*
◆ restaurant & motel   Tour 18

to Roanoke

Blue Ridge Parkway

The Blue Ridge Parkway
in Rockbridge County: 55 miles

A treasure of the National Park Service, the Blue Ridge Parkway stretches for 469 miles along the crest of the Appalachians, from the southern tip of Shenandoah National Park at Waynesboro, Virginia, to the Great Smokies in North Carolina. For about 55 miles it winds in and out of the eastern edge of Rockbridge County, where it offers spectacular views of the valley and its landmark mountains, as well as hiking trails, waterfalls, picnic places, and other delights along the road itself.

In late spring, when the rhododendron and mountain laurel dress the parkway in pastel blooms, and in October, when autumn foliage transforms the mountains, the road can become crowded, especially on weekends. In winter and early spring, the road may be closed because of fog, ice, or snow conditions that do not affect the lower elevations.

The restaurant and gas station at Whetstone Ridge, the restaurant and campground at Otter Creek, and the snack bar at the James River are open from May through October. The restaurant at the Peaks of Otter is open year-round. Maps and brochures detailing the parkway's attractions are available at the Lexington Visitor Center, the US Forest Service offices, and on the parkway itself.

Our tours describe five ways to get onto the parkway from Lexington, listed here north to south. *The distance indicated is from Lexington to the access point.*

VA 56 (Tye River Turnpike) (Tours 1, 2, or 3): US 11 (Main Street in Lexington) north to Steele's Tavern, then via VA 56 to the parkway (24 miles).

US 60 (Midland Trail) (Tour 7): US 60 (Nelson Street in Lexington) east through Buena Vista (12 miles).

VA 130 (Wert Faulkner Highway) (Tour 11): US 11 south to Natural Bridge, then east on VA 130 and south on US 501 to parkway; or **US 501 (Glasgow Highway)** (Tour 9): US 60 east to Buena Vista, then US 501 south to parkway.
  (US 501 and VA 130 share the same roadway through the James River water gap, then split again near Snowden. US 501 joins the parkway just south of the James River Visitor Center; VA 130 enters near the Otter Creek campground, about three miles north (either way, about 25 miles).

I-81 and VA 43 Take I-81 south to the US 11/Buchanan exit, then turn left onto US 11. Cross the river and turn left onto VA 43 to enter the parkway just south of the Peaks of Otter (about 40 miles). VA 43 is steep and curvy, not recommended for trailers or motor homes.

Parkway distances are clearly marked by mileposts; the location given beside each of the attractions that we describe refers to those mileposts.

In addition to the overlooks noted below, there are many other spots designated for parking that provide delightful strolls and pretty views. There are no restrooms or water fountains at any of these spots.

27.2   Access via Tye River Turnpike (VA 56) from Steele's Tavern (Tour 1), Vesuvius (Tour 2), or Irish Creek (Tour 3).

29.0   **Whetstone Ridge** Restaurant, gift shop, and gas station (open May through October), located near the headwaters of Irish Creek.

34.4   **Yankee Horse Ridge** This spot may have been named for a Union soldier's hard-ridden horse that fell and had to be shot here. A short woodland trail leads to the delightful Wigwam Falls and a reconstructed spur and trestle of the logging railroad that once climbed the mountainside.

38.8   **Boston Knob Parking Area** for a leg-stretcher trail, a tenth of a mile of easy walking, and picnic tables.

45.6   **Midland Trail (US 60)** to Lexington via Buena Vista (Tour 7).

        Sidetrip: Exit US 60E and go .3 mile to the DAR Constitution Forest on right. Established in 1938 with the planting of five Norway spruce at roadside to honor the five Virginia signers of the Constitution, this conservation project for the James River basin now comprises a bird and wildlife refuge on 45 acres of red and white pine.

45.7   Overlook with a view of **Buena Vista.** The elevation here is 2,325 feet; the valley floor is 1,500 feet below.

47.5   **Indian Gap Trail** to Indian Rocks (a third of a mile, moderately strenuous). The huge rocks perch atop a hill, out of sight of the road. Geologists tell us these rocks were not deposited here but were hidden until erosion gradually exposed them, a process that is still taking place.

49.3   **House Mountain Overlook,** elevation 2,498 feet. The view is spectacular, even by parkway standards. On a clear day you can readily identify House Mountain, Brushy Hill, Hogback, and Jump mountains (from left to right).

52.0 **Bluff Mountain Tunnel** Six hundred thirty feet long, this is the parkway's only tunnel in Virginia.

55.2 **White Oak Flats Trail** Park here for a leg-stretcher, just one tenth of a mile of easy walking beside Dancing Creek.

60.8 **Otter Creek** (May to October). Here you'll find a spacious sylvan campground, a gift shop and gas station, hiking trails, a lake to fish in, and a restaurant with a reputation for its pancakes, but no otters. They disappeared long ago.

61.2 **VA 130** Lexington via VA 130/US 501 through the James River water gap and US 60 through Buena Vista (about 25 miles). See Tours 9 or 11.

63.6 **James River Visitor Center** A ten-minute self-guided walking tour crosses the James River on a sturdy footbridge to a set of restored locks from the James River and Kanawha Canal. The 30-minute Trail of Trees takes you to the James River overlook; the trees in the hardwood-hemlock forest are identified with signs. Waterfowl, hawks, and songbirds migrate through here, and you can see one of the few cliff swallow colonies in the region from the walkway. A large picnic area overlooks the river; charcoal and wood fires are permitted in the cooking pits.

63.9 **US 501** Lexington via US 501/VA 130 and US 60 through Buena Vista. See Tours 9 or 11.

[Note: US 501 is the southernmost exit for direct return to Lexington. From here the parkway swings to the east, away from Rockbridge, then swings back into our county farther south. The next exit is VA 43 to I-81 in Buchanan, about 30 miles south.]

71.0 **Petite's Gap** Long before roads permitted travel by wagon and carriage, Thomas Jefferson and his two granddaughters rode on horseback between his home at Poplar Forest in Amherst County and the Natural Bridge. They crossed the Blue Ridge here, at Petite's Gap.

A US Forest Service road descends into Arnold's Valley (Tour 12). The road is one lane with pullouts and is not paved. Just a few yards from the parking area, this road intersects the Appalachian Trail. Park here to stroll along part of this well-marked and well-maintained hiking trail.

74.7 **Thunder Ridge Overlook** A relatively flat ten-minute loop trail leads to a very nice view of Arnold's Valley.

78.3 Overlook on **Apple Orchard Mountain** At 3,950 feet, this is the parkway's highest point in Virginia. The "apple trees" are actually Northern Red Oaks (rare in Virginia), twisted and stunted by the wind so that they resemble an apple orchard.

79.7 **Onion Mountain Overlook** A six-minute loop trail and picnic tables with views to the east.

83.1 Parking area for a mile-and-a-half loop trail to **Fallingwater Cascades.** This westward trail is somewhat rugged and rocky, but well worth the effort.

83.5 Trailhead for **Flat Top Trail,** 2.6 miles to the summit.

85.6 **Peaks of Otter** Visitor center, lodge, year-round restaurant, and gift shop overlooking a lake; camping, hiking trails. In season, a shuttle bus will carry you up Sharp Top (3,875 feet), one of the twin peaks.

91.0 **VA 43** Lexington via US 11 through Buchanan, then north on I-81.

Directory

Community Service Groups

Buena Vista Chamber of Commerce	261-2880
2202 Magnolia Avenue, Buena Vista, VA 24416	
Lexington/Rockbridge Chamber of Commerce	463-5375
10 East Washington Street, Lexington, VA 24450	
Lexington Visitor Center	463-3777
102 East Washington Street, Lexington, VA 24450	
Rockbridge Area Economic Development Commission	463-7346
6 South Randolph Street, Lexington, VA 24450	

General Information
(Books, Maps, Conversation)

The Best Seller Bookstore	463-4647
29 West Nelson Street, Lexington, VA 24450	
The Bookery	464-3377
107 West Nelston Street, Lexington, VA 24450	
The Book Store	463-8634
Washington & Lee University, Lexington, VA 24450	
Buena Vista Public Library	261-2715
2110 Magnolia Avenue, Buena Vista, VA 24416	
The General Store	261-3860
2522 Beech Avenue, Buena Vista, VA 24416	
Lexington Historical Shop	463-2615
College Square Shopping Center	
P.O. Box 1428, Lexington, VA 24450	
Rockbridge Historical Society	464-1058
Washington at Randolph, Lexington	
P.O. Box 514, Lexington, VA 24450	
Rockbridge Regional Library	463-4324
138 South Main Street, Lexington, VA 24450	
Second Story Books	463-6264
College Square Shopping Center	
P.O. Box 1384, Lexington, VA 24450	
VMI Museum Shop	464-7232
Virginia Military Institute, Lexington, VA 24450	

Local Publications

The News-Gazette and The Weekender	463-3113
20 West Nelson Street, Lexington, VA 24450	
The Rockbridge Advocate	463-2062
9 East Washington, Lexington, VA 24450	

Entertainment and Attractions

Blue Ridge Parkway
    James River Visitor Center   804-299-5941
    Otter Creek Campground   703-299-5125
    Peaks of Otter Lodge & Restaurant   800-542-5927
    Peaks of Otter Visitor Center   703-586-4357
    Whetstone Ridge Visitor Center   804-377-6397
Buffalo Springs Herb Farm   348-1083
    Raphine, VA 24472
James River Basin Canoe Livery   261-7334
    Route 4, Box 125, Lexingnton, VA 24450
Lake Robertson Recreation Park   (Headquarters) 463-4164
    Route 2, Box 251, Lexington, VA 24450   (Pool) 463-9893
Natural Bridge of Virginia
    Caverns   291-2121
    Village (hotel/gift shop)   291-2121
    Wax Museum   291-2426
Natural Bridge Zoo   291-2420
    P.O. Box 88, Natural Bridge, VA 24578
Rockbridge Winery   377-6204
    Raphine, VA 24472
Theater at Lime Kiln   463-3074
    14 South Randolph (P.O. Box 663), Lexington, VA 24450
United States Forest Service
    Cave Mountain Lake Recreation Area (phone connected May-October)   291-2745
        P.O. Box 10, Natural Bridge Station, VA 24579
    George Washington National Forest
        Pedlar District Ranger Station   261-6105
        2424 Magnolia Avenue, Buena Vista, VA 24416
    Jefferson National Forest
        Glenwood Ranger Station   291-2188
        P.O. Box 10, Natural Bridge Station, VA 24579
Wade's Mill   348-1400
    Raphine, VA 24472

Emergency Numbers

Dial 911 or the following numbers:
    Buena Vista Police Department   261-6171
    Lexington Police Department   463-2112
    Rockbridge County Sheriff   463-7328
    Virginia State Police   (Emergencies only) 800-542-5959

    Stonewall Jackson Hospital   463-9141

For Further Reading

Appalachian Trail Guide to Central and Southwest Virginia. Harpers Ferry: Appalachian Trail Conference, 1988.

Henry Boley, *Lexington in Old Virginia.* Richmond: Garrett & Massie, 1936; Lexington: Liberty Hall Press, Washington & Lee University, 1974; Natural Bridge Station: Rockbridge Publishing Co., 1991.

Stan Cohen, *Historic Springs of the Virginias.* Charleston, West Virginia: Pictorial Histories Publishing Company, 1981.

Charles B. Dew, *Bond of Iron: Master and Slave at Buffalo Forge.* New York: W. W. Norton & Co., 1994.

Field Guide to the Chessie Nature Trail, ed. by Larry I. Bland. Lexington: Rockbridge Area Conservation Council, 1988.

Keith Frye, *Roadside Geology of Virginia.* Missoula: Mountain Press, 1986.

Winifred Hadsel, *Roads of Rockbridge.* Lexington: Rockbridge Historical Society, 1993.

Winifred Hadsel, *The Streets of Lexington.* Lexington: Rockbridge Historical Society, 1985.

Anne McCorkle Knox, *Gentle Ghosts.* Lexington: Brandon Publishing Company, 1981.

John Seymour Letcher, *Only Yesterday in Lexington, Virginia.* Verona, Virginia: McClure Press, 1974, 1976.

James G. Leyburn, *The Scotch-Irish.* Chapel Hill: University of North Carolina Press, 1962.

William G. Lord, *Blue Ridge Parkway Guide: Rockfish Gap to Roanoke.* Yorktown: Eastern Acorn Press, 1981.

Royster Lyle, Jr., and Pamela Hemenway Simpson, *The Architecture of Historic Lexington.* Charlottesville: University of Virginia Press, 1977.

James W. McClung, *Historical Significance of Rockbridge County, Virginia.* Staunton: McClure Co., 1939.

Oren F. Morten, *A History of Rockbridge County, Virginia*. Baltimore, Regional Publishing Co;, 1920, 1980.

One Hundred Historic Sites and Structures in Rockbridge County. Lexington: Association for the Preservation of Virginia Antiquities, 1979.

Proceedings of the Rockbridge Historical Society. Volumes I (1939-1941) through IX (1982). Lexington: Rockbridge Historical Society.

A Brief History of Public Education in Rockbridge County, Lexington, Buena Vista 1748-1980. Lexington: Rockbridge Retired Teachers Association, 1980.

Edmund Pendleton Tompkins, *Rockbridge County, Virginia: An Informal History*. Richmond: Whittet & Shepperson, 1952.

Virginia Cemeteries, ed. by Anne M. Hogg with Dennis A. Tosh. Charlottesville: University of Virginia Press, 1986.

Gary C. Walker, *Yankee Soldiers in Virginia Valleys: Hunter's Raid*. Roanoke: A & W Enterprise, 1989.

Klaus Wust, *The Virginia Germans*. Charlottesville: University Press of Virginia, 1969.

Index

Index

Walnut Grove Farm 34
Washington & Lee University 3, 79
Washington, George 67, 97
Washington, Lawrence 64
Weaver, William 53
Welsh, Sally Grigsby 64
Welsh, Thomas II 64
Whetstone Ridge restaurant 17
White Oaks Flat Trail 120

Wilburn, W.R. 31
Wilson Springs 23
Wilson, Robert 106
Wilson, William A. II 23
woolen industry 112

Y
Yankee Horse Ridge 119